THE
LOVER
WITHIN

THE LOVER WITHIN

Accessing the Lover in the Male Psyche

ROBERT MOORE & DOUGLAS GILLETTE

AVON BOOKS ◆ NEW YORK

Permissions, constituting a continuation of this copyright page, appear on pages 287-288.

AVON BOOKS
A division of
The Hearst Corporation
1350 Avenue of the Americas
New York, New York 10019

Copyright © 1993 by Douglas Gillette and Robert Moore
Published by arrangement with William Morrow and Company, Inc.
Library of Congress Catalog Card Number: 92-46193
ISBN: 0-380-72071-X

The William Morrow edition contains the following Library of Congress Cataloging in Publication Data:
Moore, Robert L.
  The lover within: accessing the lover in the male psyche / by Robert Moore and Douglas Gillette.
    p.   cm.
1. Men—Psychology. 2. Masculinity (Psychology). 3. Sex role. 4. Archetype (Psychology). I. Gillette, Douglas. II. Title.
BF692.5.M655   1993   92-46193
155.3'32—dc20   CIP

First Avon Books Trade Printing: February 1995

AVON TRADEMARK REG. U.S. PAT. OFF. AND IN OTHER COUNTRIES, MARCA REGISTRADA, HECHO EN U.S.A.

Printed in the U.S.A.

OPM 10 9 8 7 6 5 4 3 2 1

To artists, writers, musicians, dreamers, mystics, and all those men who have brought masculine love and joy to their families and friends, their tribes and nations, and to all inhabitants of their home planet. May they continue to foster a wider understanding of truth, justice, and beauty.

"Thou *art* that!"

A Hindu affirmation that recognizes our oneness with all others and
with all things

EROTIC MAN AND THE GARDEN OF LOVE

"TAKE MY HAND, I'M A STRANGER IN PARA-
dise," sings the love-struck prince of Baghdad in the
musical *Kismet*. He is standing at the center of his lush palace
garden, where birds are singing in fruit-laden trees, and water
is splashing in a marble fountain. Somewhere beyond the
confines of his glorious garden, in the bustling city he hardly
knows, lives his beloved. He cries out, "I'm a stranger in
paradise, lost in a wonderland . . . Somewhere in space, I hang
suspended until I know there's a chance that you care." He
finds himself "out of the commonplace" and lifted into "the
rare." Calling to his "other half," his "lost self," he asks her

to "answer the fervent prayer of this stranger in paradise, and tell him that he need be a stranger no more."

The song is set in the Garden of Delight, a garden well known to any man of any time or place who has been deeply in love—with life, ideals, God, or most especially with a woman. It is the place where a wish made upon the first star that sparkles through the enchanted foliage can actually make dreams come true; it is the Eden from which we believe we have been expelled.

The collective human psyche remembers the Garden as the place in which we dwelled before forsaking the dreaming innocence of animals in favor of greater consciousness. We knew there what it was like to be embraced by the rapturous arms of the archetypal Lover, and we anticipate being embraced there again, outside of our workaday lives of "quiet desperation." This is the sacred space we are propelled into when we fall in love. And when we fall out of love, we relive the same devastation Adam and Eve felt at their original, mythical expulsion from the Garden. We also experience their insatiable hunger to return.

The longing for the transcendent ecstasy found in Eden is, for many men, more powerful than any other. As our songs remind us, we would prefer to give up fame and fortune—even sometimes life and limb—to spend an eternal moment in the Garden, enjoying the aroma of our beloved.

There are means by which we can enjoy the libidinal energies of the Lover without becoming possessed by him. In this book we will explore how to allow ourselves time in the Lover's Garden, without having to abandon our lives and livelihoods to get there. We are each entitled to the energy of the Lover, for he does not reside far from us—his Garden of Love is within.

Those readers who are new to this series will find in Chapters 1 and 2 a basic grounding in the Jungian concepts we

have extended in this work. In the three Appendices we expand, for the interested reader, on some intriguing structural
aspects of the psyche that lend support to our work. These two
chapters and the three appendices are common to all four
books in this series. Thus the new reader can find all the basic
information he needs in any single book. The reader familiar
with another book in the series may choose to turn directly to
Chapter 3.

With the publication of this book our five-volume series
on masculine psychology is complete and available as a re-
source for men seeking masculine maturity and empowerment. Our hope is that through this series men around the
world may be enabled to access more adequately the four
instinctual cornerstones of mature masculinity. We believe
that the vision presented in these books is the distillation of
the essential *normative* vision of those generative men who
have sought to live out the best and the fullest expression of
the male gender throughout the history of our species. This
vision represents the male blueprint for the kind of generativity that, realized in the lives of individual men and in their
societies, will write a new chapter in the natural history of our
planet. Without the empowerment of men for greater gender-
characteristic maturity this new chapter cannot be written.
But by grasping this vision and living it, it is still possible for
us to secure the fulfillment of our species' potential.

ACKNOWLEDGMENTS

THE AUTHORS WISH TO THANK GLADYS RIOS AND Graciela Infante for their reflections on the early form of the manuscript. Doug especially wishes to express his appreciation for their wisdom and encouragement.

Robert wants to express especial appreciation to Margaret Shanahan for her inspiration and encouragement since the days when many of these ideas were being formulated initially as lectures. Since 1985 her ongoing companionship and support have not only stimulated his work but deeply enriched his life and his understanding of the four powers of the psyche.

Both authors wish to thank Patrick Nugent and Angela Smith for their transcriptions of Robert Moore's lecture tapes, Noel Kaufmann for his location of research sources, Max Havlick, Perry Cartwright, and Dong Chamberlin for their work on permissions and bibliography, and Rudy Vetter for his excellent photography.

Special thanks go to Maria Guarnaschelli (vice president and senior editor at William Morrow) for her innovative vision for this series and for her intensive and superlative editorial work. Chas Edwards has been tireless in his ongoing liaison work and in his commitment to effective coordination and getting all the details together for preparation of the manuscript. Kurt Aldag has given his insights into how best to communicate the ideas in this book to the widest audience. These and the other outstanding Morrow staff have made the success of this book possible.

In addition, the authors wish to acknowledge the many men, inside and outside of the men's movement, who have reflected on their personal experience as men and helped refine the understanding of the four powers and four masculine initiations presented in this series of books. With their continuing help, perhaps these masculine powers can be accessed in more helpful and generative ways to serve the human community.

CONTENTS

PART 4
EROTIC MAN:
EMBODYING MASCULINE JOY

APPENDICES

"Thou art that!"
—A Hindu proverb which affirms
the oneness of all beings

THE
LOVER
WITHIN

PART 1

HARD WIRING:
THE MASCULINE
SOUL

1

GENDER IDENTITY, GENDER ASYMMETRY, AND THE SEXUAL IMBALANCE OF POWER

INCREASINGLY TODAY, MEN AND WOMEN ARE STRUG-gling to live in a twilight world of gender confusion. Anxiously they wonder what, if anything, constitutes their own unique sexual identity. Women don business suits and become bankers and lawyers. Men clean house and learn to change diapers. These shifts in traditional work roles may be all to the good. But are there any real differences between men and women? If not, what joy is left us in sexual union? Have we become interchangeable parts, androgynous to the core?

Some teach us to feel ashamed of our sex-specific differences. Supporters of radical androgyny go so far as to discourage research into the dissimilarities in brain structure, or in the chemical, hormonal, or instinctual configurations that may influence some culturally exaggerated scripts.[1]

Some theorists offer stereotyped ideals of "feminine" psychological characteristics, now alone deemed fully human.[2] Boys are said to be developmentally inferior to girls. Men are held to be biologically and emotionally inferior to women. Some radical feminists assert women would be better off without men entirely—or that male children should be genetically or socially engineered to eliminate "masculine aggressiveness."

This is not to say that all feminist criticism is invalid. The feminist critique of patriarchal societies makes a great deal of sense. Patriarchy *does* tend to institutionalize a particular kind of masculinity, prone to exploiting and oppressing other human beings, other species, and the environment. But oppressive, "macho" societies deny *men* their mature masculinity as certainly as they degrade women and feminine attributes. Typically a small minority of underdeveloped males at the top of the social pyramid will control power and wealth to the exclusion of all others, male and female. They rank these others in a descending order of usefulness to themselves and defend against them with all the force of their inflated self-regard. Patriarchy is therefore a manifestation of the infantile grandiosity suffered by its leaders.

Patriarchy is set up and run not for men as a gender or for masculinity in its fullness or in its mature expressions but rather by men who are fundamentally *immature*. It is really the rule of boys, often cruel and abusive boys. For the most part, we believe human societies have always consisted of boys and girls more or less unconsciously acting out their immature and grandiose fantasies. Our planetary home more often than not has resembled the island world in William Golding's *Lord of the Flies*. Thus our societies have, on the whole, opposed the realization and expression of *both* mature feminine and masculine psyches.

Brutalized children—and for most children in most times and places brutality is a commonplace—become brutal adults. But they are not really adults. They can only pretend to be adults while they still operate on a level of childish self-aggrandizement. The developmental crippling that generates patriarchy is not however the sole responsibility of childish males. Immature males *and* females are unconscious partners in the socially sanctioned repression of children. A child's sense of self is distorted by a mother who fails to confront her own emotional issues, and her own unresolved needs for power and adulation. The therapist Alice Miller has written a pioneering series of books that addresses poisonous pedagogy,[3] as she calls this problem. Childish men and women never outgrow being self-interested and self-involved, and they pass their own wounds on to their children. Mature men and women find the ways to be selfless in their regard for others, even as they are manifestly self-caring.

In sum, we feel it is wrong to view patriarchy as the expression of a mature masculinity or of masculinity in its essence. Patriarchal societies are out of balance partly because at their helm are unbalanced men. And while we abhor the often horrific abuses of patriarchal systems, we also remember that males helped generate, from earlier urban neolithic cultures, all the higher civilizations we know from recorded history.[4] The efforts of dynamic, life-engendering men have left an astounding record of discovery and achievement. Clearly the energies of men, in partnership with women and their feminine energies, have fueled (and will continue to fuel) the significant advances of imagination and social organization that characterize our species. Men of the past, in every tribe and nation, have struggled to learn how to use their power to bless the human community. We continue to struggle today.

Lost in Childhood:
Failed Initiation (Egyptian figure of mourning)

Defining masculine and feminine characteristics has led to much discussion. After years of research, depth psychologists and others argue that each sex carries both the psychological and physical traits of the other.[5] No man is purely masculine, just as there is no purely feminine woman.[6] Jungian psychologists call the feminine characteristics of the male psyche the Anima; the female psyche's masculine characteristics they call the Animus.

Both the Animus and the Anima develop in complex fashion as the personality grows to maturity. Neither men nor women can reach psychological maturity without integrating their respective contrasexual other. A man's female elements enhance his manhood, just as a woman's male aspects enhance her womanhood. Typically masculine characteristics are dominant in a man, as are feminine characteristics in a woman. Of course there are exceptions, but this is usually the case. Central to all these discussions is the question of whether masculinity is in its *essence* more coercive, more abusive of power, more compulsively dominance-seeking than femininity. Many have implied or argued that biological gender differences *necessitate* rigid sex-role differentiation and make masculine dominance *inevitable*.

For example, the changing history of male and female roles within the Israeli kibbutzim are presented as evidence of innate masculine and feminine characteristics.[7] The kibbutzim were founded as farming communities in the late nineteenth century under the influence of Marxist ideals. Men and women were viewed not only as equal, but as inherently the same. In the fields, women worked the same long hours as the men. In the kitchens, nurseries, and children's dormitories men worked the same long hours as the women.

As the years passed, however, an unexpected development occurred. Slowly the women left the fields, the traditional areas of men's work. More and more they specialized in the work of the kitchens, nurseries, and dormitories. Gradually, the men specialized in the field work. Against the enormous pressure of kibbutz ideology most men and women sorted themselves into "traditional" gender-specific roles. Was this the result of biology or immature manipulation of masculine power? According to sociobiology, primate ethology, and brain-structure/hormonal research, there *may* be instinctual biological roots for such tendencies in social behavior.[8] In addition, the anthropologist David Gilmore, in his *Manhood in the Making*—the first extensively documented cross-cultural examination of the "cult of manhood"—strongly indicates a widespread societal support for a division of social and work roles among men and women.[9]

Even if it could be proved, however, that some traditionally masculine or feminine *tendencies* may be inherited this would not be a basis for justifying the usual caricatures of these traits. Above all, it does not justify the assumption that men are inherently violent, inordinately aggressive, insensitive, and uninterested in intimate relationships, nor that women have a monopoly on gentle, nurturing, emotional, and intuitive behaviors. Probably the most accurate argument is that men are more "hard-wired" for some psychological tendencies and women for others. Unfortunately, historical cultures nearly always have amplified rather than helped us compensate for these tendencies.

Important as all these considerations may be, in this book our purpose is not to focus on gender difference. We intend rather to advance understanding of the deep masculine and the challenge of stewarding masculine power. *For whatever the source of masculine abuse of power, it is our responsibility as contemporary men to understand it and to develop the emotional and spiritual resources to end it.* We want to help men express what psychoanalyst Erik Erikson termed the "generative man" within themselves.[10] We will do this by exploring how masculinity is anchored in the place where body, instinct, mind, and soul arise in men.

Contrary to those thinkers who, with Reinhold Niebuhr, regard power itself as inevitably leading to evil,[11] we believe it is possible to steward power responsibly. The drive toward attaining personal and corporate empowerment is as much a part of our instinctual makeup as eating, sleeping, and procreating. We cannot wish away what psychologist Alfred Adler called the "will to power,"[12] the desire to overcome. "We shall overcome" is not just a civil-rights rallying cry—it is a human instinct to achieve efficacy and competence in adaptation. We cannot and should not raise our children to eschew this primal and ultimately life-enhancing instinct.[13] The issue should never be how to get rid of the urge for power, masculine or feminine. The real issue is how to steward it, and how to channel our other instincts along with it into life-giving and world-building activities.

THE PROBLEM OF THE MODERN ATTACK ON MYTH AND RITUAL

The creative use of instinctual male energies, like the good use of any energy source, requires maturity. Human maturity has probably always been a rare commodity. But we believe it was, at least in some respects, more available in the past than it is today. It was more available even in patriarchal states, with all of their drawbacks, than it is in our modern societies. In the past there were powerful rites of initiation presided over by ritual elders to help boys and girls remake themselves into men and women capable of assuming their social responsibilities.[14] The scope of these premodern initiation rituals was often limited by inflexible cultural norms. But they did provide boys and girls with workable blueprints for achieving gender-specific maturity and were based on mythic visions of the tribe's view of the best in human nature—their normative vision of the possible human.

An apprentice electrician must be initiated by an experienced master into the mysteries of electricity's sources, methods of generation, and technologies of distribution. Whatever the apprentice does not take care to understand is a danger to him, because electricity carries force enough to kill him. In similar fashion all human beings need to be initiated into the wise and life-enhancing uses of human psychological resources. Where misunderstood, the energies of our psyches can wreak havoc upon our lives. Despite the elaborate training our modern society provides an individual mastering a trade, we do not think to offer anything similar to the man who wishes to master his own psyche. But our lack of teachers doesn't change our need to learn how to access the powerful energies of our deep souls.

Essentially, the process of initiation removes our Ego from the center of the universe. When a society abandons initiation rituals, individual Egos lose an appropriate means of learning this valuable lesson. Life circumstances will urge the same lesson upon the Ego eventually, but perhaps in a very painful, inopportune manner. But by far the most serious consequence of ceasing initiatory practices is the loss of a periodic social forum for considering the nature of maturity. A society has to know what maturity is before it can pass the knowledge on. It's as if we no longer have a map to get us to maturity. If you don't know where something is, and you don't have a map, how do you get there? A few will stumble across the destination. But most of us end up getting hopelessly lost. When people bemoan our culture's loss of values, in part they are missing the old transformative rituals—for rituals provide a structure within which social values can be recalled and reconsidered.

In many tribal societies initiation ceremonies are still given the prominence they deserve. Through ritual training and the special imparting of carefully stewarded wisdom, the Ego is displaced into an orbital position around a Transpersonal Other. The Ego may experience this Transpersonal Other as any kind of group or task to which the individual pledges his or her loyalties, best efforts, even his or her life. In premodern societies, such group tasks and loyalties are always themselves ultimately subordinate to and given meaning by a greater Transpersonal Other, which religions of the world call "God."

As a complete cultural system, modernity has largely turned its back on God, on effective processes of initiation, on ritual elders, and even on family, tribe, and nation. Consequently, an individual Ego can no longer reach the sober but joyous realization of its *non*central position in the psyche and in the wider universe. Nature fills the vacuum modernity has created with our modern Egos, which expand terrifically to fill the empty space. Where a powerful Transpersonal Other is missing, God is replaced by unconscious pretensions to godhood.

An individual psyche, bloated by dangerously distorted assessments of self and others around it—family, friends, lovers, company, nation, and perhaps the entire globe—must pay the price for its infantilism. Corrupt politicians, money-hungry yuppies, drug dealers, wife (and husband) abusers, and new racists are but a few examples of infantilism run amok. Petty dictators, self-styled fundamentalist "messiahs" and their terrorist henchmen, Khmer Rouge genocidal murderers, Chinese Communist–party bullies, irresponsible international oil company executives, among many others, cause the social and environmental devastation that always accompanies the

Ego inflation of the human psyche unchecked by a sense of limits grounded in a Transpersonal Other. These would-be men and women have failed to grasp a sufficiently wide and deep vision of the archetypal realities upon which our psyche is founded. It is time we look again to these deep structures and draw from them the psychic support our era so desperately needs.

2

DECODING THE MALE
PSYCHE

C ARL GUSTAV JUNG FOUNDED THE SCHOOL OF AN-
alytical or "depth" psychology that provides the overall
framework of our work.[1] We also rely heavily on insights from
theorists of other schools such as Sigmund Freud, Erik Erikson, D. W. Winnicott, Heinz Kohut, and Alice Miller. But we
believe Jung's approach is the only one to provide a truly
transcultural understanding of the human psyche. His is also
the only approach to adequately bridge the gap between modern science and the mythological and spiritual traditions of
our species.

Jungian depth psychology values the mysteries of the

human soul. Dreams, visions, symbols, images, and cultural achievements arise from those mysterious depths that the world's religions understand as the "spiritual dimension." Depth psychology embraces all human experience as authentic to the psyche. Consequently, phenomena such as the "soul," "demonic possession," "revelation," "prayer," or "god" are completely compatible with scientific truth. Because all experiences are psychological, all are real, no matter how strange.[2] Above all, *any* human experience is both *based on* and *perceived by* the deep psychological structures within us.[3]

Before we explore the deep structures of the male psyche, it will be helpful to define a few Jungian terms.

MYTH: For depth psychologists myth does not imply a naïve, untrue, prescientific tale about the origins of the world or humankind. Myths are true stories that describe the ways of the psyche and the means by which our psychological energies interact.[4] Myths project our inner dynamics onto the outer world and allow us to experience it through the filter of how we think and feel.[5]

Since in a real sense we *are* the universe and the universe is us, myths often accurately describe the workings of the larger universe by using anthropomorphic images. That is to say, we are products of the universe in the same way that galaxies, oceans, and trees are. It would be a very strange thing indeed if our psyche did not mirror the structures found outside in the cosmos. An immediate and intimate correspondence between *inner* and *outer* is fundamental to our nature as beings. If no such link existed, we would be unable to acquire any realistic or workable knowledge of the world. We would be unable to survive. Ultimately, it is possible that *inner* and *outer* are purely subjective, pragmatic distinctions made by our consciousness in order to navigate within a mystery it cannot fully fathom.

Creation myths illustrate this beautifully. In the Bible, the Hebrew God Yahweh creates the material world by speaking. He says, "Let there be such and such!" and there is such and such. Behind this concept of creation stands the idea that naming something brings it into existence. Of course, modern science maintains the world did not come into being through a divine uttering of words or the naming of material objects. The biblical account does not convey a scientific truth about the world's origin. The truth it speaks is psychological.

Human consciousness at its height is developed largely by the mastering of words. Arising from language, at the same time it gives rise *to* language, consciousness creates our experience as it defines creation. The words we use for things allow us to distinguish *this* from *that*. They also profoundly color how we think and feel about those things. What we cannot name is therefore not fully real or fully experienced for us. As far as our psyche is concerned, an unnamed thing is "uncreated."[6] Thus the biblical image of Yahweh creating the world by naming it is true to human psychological processes. At the same time, if we assume there is an intelligence behind the created world, it might be true that that intelligence manifested the universe through some process analogous to the human use of language. If this were so, the biblical story would be working both as a psychological parable and as a visionary expression of a process that really *is* occurring in the universe as a whole.

EGO: When Jungian psychoanalysts talk about the Ego, they usually mean the "I" we normally think of as ourselves.[7] The Ego is who we believe ourselves to be, the part of our psyche we identify with our name. When we say, "*I* feel this way about something," or "*I* think I'll do that," the Ego is probably speaking. Jungian theorists sometimes define the Ego as a *complex*. By this they mean a structural element of the total psyche that exhibits certain specific features. The Ego operates in what we imagine to be our capacity to think rationally, in our feelings, in our ability to will actions, remember the past, and create the future, and in our encounter with consciousness.

In reality, however, the question of the Ego is more complicated. Often "I" am not the one who is thinking, feeling, acting, willing, or deciding. Rather some *autonomous complex* other than the Ego may temporarily "possess" it and make it operate out of the complex's perspective. Since the Ego is largely unaware of these other complexes, it is tricked into the illusory feeling of holding a solitary place in the psyche, and into an accompanying illusion of its "free will." According to Jung, the other complexes operate largely from the personal unconscious, but may also be anchored in a transpersonal unconscious which exerts a deeper influence on the psyche.

CONSCIOUSNESS: Consciousness is not confined to the Ego. The *sub*conscious or *un*conscious is itself conscious. It is only unconscious—invisible and indistinct—from the *Ego*'s perspective.[8] Personal complexes other than the Ego, and the deeper transpersonal psychological structures of the unconscious, can be conscious of each other and of the Ego, and they operate out of their own agendas. The case of multiple-personality disorder demonstrates this clearly. Here highly activated complexes usurp the place of the Ego in the daily affairs of the afflicted person, causing him or her to behave in ways the Ego neither wishes nor sometimes even remembers afterward.

What is true for people who suffer multiple-personality disorder is true, though to a lesser extent, for all of us. We all at times act in ways contrary to how our Ego wills us to behave, perhaps through deep mood swings and emotionally violent outbursts of fear and rage. When we return to a state of Ego consciousness, we say such things as "I went out of my head" or "I don't know what came over me." What came over us, like a wave of energy that shifted our whole mode of perceiving, feeling, and acting, was an autonomous complex, another consciousness from within the total psychic system that is our Self.

Autonomous complexes are usually (though not always) organized around traumatic childhood experiences.[9] During early traumas, our emerging Egos split off and repressed aspects of the psyche that parents, siblings, or society found unacceptable. These split-off aspects could be thoughts, feelings, images, or associations. Often they are valuable and worth recall. They may carry hidden talents, intuitions, abilities, or accurate feelings that would make our personalities wiser and more complete if we could reintegrate them. Until reintegration can occur, our psyches are like the pieces of a broken mirror, which hold in fragments what was once a complete reflection. Through all our complexes, including the Ego, and the vast territory of the unconscious, consciousness pervades our psyche.

ARCHETYPES: Archetypes operate at a level of the psyche deeper than that of the personal unconscious with its autonomous complexes. They are the hard-wired components of our genetically transmitted psychic machine.[10] They are the bedrock structures that define the human psyche's own nature, and make it the same, regardless of the culture in which an individual lives. In this sense archetypes represent transpersonal human psychological characteristics. They are dynamic, energic elements in all of us. They well up and fall deep within our unconscious like tidal pulls. Our daily life is influenced by these energies in ways we can never fully understand.

Jung declared that the archetypes are equivalent to the instincts of other animals. He located them in what he called the *collective unconscious*.[11] The existence of an unconscious, or what many called the subconscious, had been noted for some time. But Freud was the first to make it the focus of major psychological investigation. Before him, even where psychologists acknowledged the subconscious mind's existence, they usually dismissed it as an inert repository of forgotten or repressed experiences.

Freud's interest in the mind's possibilities had been aroused during his medical studies with the great Parisian hypnotist, Jean Martin Charcot. Charcot dismissed the results of his own experimental demonstrations as stemming from patient hysteria. Whatever their source, the hypnotic manifestations witnessed by the young Freud convinced him he'd found a rich field for further study.

Common to all of us, Freud's life work implied, was a subconscious deeper than a particular personal one. He called this instinctually based subconscious the *Id* (the Latin word for "it").[12] This wild, primitive Id was responsible for all kinds of enormously powerful and irrational impulses, especially aggressive sexuality.

Classic Freudians have tended to regard the subconscious as more or less unstructured. But a number of neo-Freudians maintain that the deep psyche, far from being chaotic, is characterized by structure. Erik Erikson talks about "instinctive structures" and "performed action patterns," which, under appropriate circumstances, call up "drive energy for instantaneous, vigorous, and skillful release."[13] He proposes the existence of "a general psychic energy (instinctual force) which can be put to use by a variety of performed and relatively autonomous instinctive patterns."[14] He also says, "the action patterns—the modes and modalities—are all present in the ground plan from the beginning, yet they have their special time of ascending."[15] His thoughts come remarkably close to the Jungian conception of time-and-circumstance-released archetypal "action patterns" from the collective unconscious.

Jung pushed the exploration of the collective unconscious structures a step further. Stored within them, he claimed,
are both the human psyche's archetypal building blocks and
the accumulated collective memory of the entire human race.
He reached this conclusion because he discovered that symbols, images, myths, and Gods from different cultures and
epochs bore striking resemblances to one another and also to
the images that appeared in his patients' dreams. According to
his conception, the collective unconscious is the source and
the limitless reservoir of all the images recorded in human art,
mythology, and religion. From it leap both the poet's song and
the scientist's insight. From it flow the signal dreams which
have implication often for an entire society as much as for
their dreamer.

The psyche's archetypal structures serve as conduits for
great charges of primal psychological energy. Because of their
own dynamic configuration, they mold this energy, imparting
to it their particular patterns. Psychologists call this life-force
in psychic form the *Libido*.[16] Freud believed that Libido is
fundamentally sexual. Any expression of the Libido redirected
into pursuits other than sexual ones he called "sublimations."
Jung, on the other hand, believed that the Libido is a general-
ized life-force that expresses itself through imaginal and spiritual impulses, as well as through sexuality.

For any individual the archetypes may be creative and
life-enhancing or destructive and death-dealing. The result
depends in part on how the Ego is able to relate to them based
on its own developmental history. Properly accessing and
using the Libido available to the psyche amount to a sort of
psychological technology. If we learn the technology and use
it properly, we can use the energy to make generative men and
women of ourselves. But if we fail to learn how to use these
vast energy resources, or misuse them, we will be courting our
own destruction, and we may take others with us. If we try to

ignore the archetypes, they exert their mighty influence upon us nonetheless. They bend us to their nonhuman, sometimes *in*human wills. We must therefore face the evidence depth psychology and other studies have provided us. We are not as free of instinct or unconscious content as we have been encouraged to believe. Genuine freedom for the Ego results from acknowledging and properly accessing the chemical fires that burn hot in our unconscious minds.

Some Jungian analysts romanticize the archetypes.[17] They encourage their patients to find and claim the particular archetype or myth that has organized their lives. Life then becomes a process of affirming and living out this myth. In our opinion our goal should not be to identify with an archetypal pattern, or to allow a mythic expression of it to make our lives what it will. We believe that when we romantically *identify* with any archetype we cease to be viable human beings moving toward wholeness. If we are drawn to an archetype by its seductive power, its promise that we can shirk our individual responsibilities and the pain involved in being a person with a personal Ego, we will be crushed by the sheer weight of unconscious compulsive impulses.

On the other hand, our goal is not to become *ordinary* in our quest for psychic health. We must not lose the vital connection with the libidinal energy the archetypes supply us so that we can live our lives fully, energetically, and creatively. Our goal is to learn how to *differentiate* ourselves from the archetypes without completely *disassociating* ourselves from them. If we learn to access them successfully, they become resources of energy both for our personal lives and for healing our planet—we become more radiant in every area of our lives.

More precisely stated, our objective is to develop mature Ego structures strong enough to channel useful libidinal energy into our daily lives. We can begin by making ourselves conscious of how archetypal energies already possess us. Only then can we begin to access them creatively, through a process that provides us with a greater sense of free will in the choices of our lives. The effort to achieve liberation for ourselves will in turn motivate us to help others do the same. Our renewed energies benefit ourselves and others on all the levels of our psychic organization: the personal, the familial, the communal, national, and global.

SHADOW: Jung himself occasionally identified the Shadow with the totality of the unconscious. But most depth psychologists view the Shadow as an individual, multifaceted contra-Ego, of the same sex as the Ego.[18] If the Ego is a photograph, the Shadow is its negative. Standing in direct opposition to the Ego, the Shadow is an autonomous complex, which holds opinions, expresses feelings, and generally wills an agenda radically different from the Ego's.

Like most autonomous complexes, the Shadow results from childhood trauma. Those qualities of a person's total psyche that are diametrically opposed to the emerging Ego, and that the Ego rejects because of the pressures of the childhood environment, coalesce in the unconscious. There they form a distinct, conscious, willing entity. Unless reintegrated later in life, they forever seek to sabotage the Ego's plans and behaviors.

We have all had the experience of willing one scenario and living quite another. For example, we intend to remain friendly while visiting our in-laws, but then find ourselves drawn irresistibly into arguments and confrontation. Our Egos want to maintain an image of family harmony. Our Shadows, unable to tolerate such hypocrisy, and feeling real animosity toward our in-laws, compel us to behave in a more honest, if more destructive, way.

The animosity we feel is ultimately toward ourselves, but

it often takes a lot of work before we can realize this. The Shadow endorses this work because it longs for reintegration. It is the Shadow's method to lead us into holding our impossibly defensive, illogical positions—in order to confront us with whatever psychic complexes we would rather forget. Our "real world" hatreds are most usually against these inner complexes, and our Shadow works by *repetition compulsion* to call our attention to them.

Rather than face any rejected qualities, either positive or negative, within ourselves, we frequently deal with our Shadow by projecting those qualities onto others.[19] As an Ego, we don't project them. But our Shadow does so in order to focus our interest on its feelings, wishes, and agendas. Our Shadow induces us to see other people we disapprove of or dislike in colors that are perhaps only marginally like their "true" colors but which *are* colors that the Shadow itself possesses.

Jung believed withdrawing a projection of the Shadow and owning it as a part of ourselves requires enormous moral courage. He also believed that what we will not face within our psyche we will be forced to confront in the outer world. So, if we can claim our Shadow's qualities, and learn from them, we defuse much of the interpersonal conflict we would otherwise encounter. People who have served as the screens for our Shadow's projections become less odious, and more human. At the same time, we experience ourselves as richer, more complex, and more powerful individuals.

THE TRIANGULAR STRUCTURE
OF THE ARCHETYPES

In this book our definition of the Shadow includes this traditional Jungian understanding, but introduces another archetypal, transpersonal aspect to it as well. We believe masculine and feminine archetypes possess their own Shadows. The King, the Warrior, the Magician, and the Lover are the masculine archetypal structures we have undertaken to study in this series. In one sense these archetypes are operating at more primitive levels than the Ego accessing them, and each has its own Shadow.

In our extended definition, a Shadow always manifests where there is an immature, fragmentary psyche, because splitting is always a symptom of unintegrated development.[20] In the traditional Jungian view of maturity, wholeness is achieved largely to the degree that the split between the Ego and the Shadow is overcome. In large part, psychological maturity is a measure of how thoroughly the Ego is able to integrate the Shadow into its consciousness.

We maintain that the Ego/Shadow split represents a Shadow system in itself. The split actually involves the Ego in the *bipolar* Shadow of one or more archetypes. In this situation our Ego usually identifies with one pole of the archetypal Shadow and disassociates from the other. In our view, then, the Shadow can still be regarded in the traditional way as the psychic area from which the Ego is divided but, more fully, as a bipolar *system* characterized by splitting, repression, and projection *within* the energy field of an archetype.

For a long time psychologists associated "bipolar disorder" almost exclusively with the manic-depressive personality.[21] Then, in his *Modern Psychopathology*, Theodore Millon extended the idea of bipolarity to include passive and active dimensions in all the major disorders of personality.[22] In a similar fashion, some Jungians have described a bipolar relationship between certain archetypes (though they are not in themselves personality disorders). That gave rise to such archetypal pairs as the senex-puer (old man—eternal boy), the domina-puella (old woman—eternal girl) and others.[23]

In the case of the Warrior archetype, for example, neither the Sadist nor the Masochist (the two poles of the Warrior's Shadow) represents personal growth or fulfillment. The full embodiment of the Warrior is to be found in a third transcending option that integrates the two poles into a creative psychological structure. Since they define psychic wholeness, archetypes always reconcile opposing forces in this way. Both of the opposing poles in the archetypal Shadow systems contain qualities essential for psychological health. But if left in their state of chronic tension, they will condemn the Ego to a fragmented and immature existence. Guided by the archetypes in their transcending fullness, a mature personality integrates these important qualities by reconciling the divisions in the archetypal Shadow.

Our refined understanding of how the archetypes work suggests interesting analogies with other schools of thought. The psychologist Alfred Adler, a contemporary of Freud and Jung, believed personality disorders appear both in active and passive modes in a way similar to our view of how archetypal Shadow systems work. The Christian theologian Paul Tillich grounded his thought with a belief in what he called the "ambiguities" of space and time in the created world. He believed that these ambiguities find their resolution in a third, higher reality "above" history.[24] The impulse to achieve this comes from the "Spirit." The German philosopher Hegel saw the forward movement of the universe as occurring through a "thesis, antithesis, synthesis" process in which each synthesis became a new thesis, and so on in a continual upward program of evolutionary complexity and integration.[25] Alfred North Whitehead, the great twentieth-century American philosopher, sees the whole "adventure of ideas," ideas that *create* the world, as a process by which God lures the created world forward in tiny increments, which he calls "occasions."[26] These occasions are like Hegel's theses, and God is the ever-changing antithesis. Whitehead calls this unceasing process "creative advance."

Similarly, Jung drew from his alchemical studies the idea of the *coniunctio oppositorum* ("union of opposites")[27] impelled by a "transcendent function"—the conceptual equivalent to Tillich's "Spirit" and Whitehead's "lure." Jung believed it is essential for the Ego to balance opposing images, feelings, and points of view without allowing either of the opposed sides to disappear into the unconscious. Eventually, when this struggle is consciously experienced with all the suffering it demands, our psyche can follow a transcendent third possibility into greater wholeness.

Jung's followers have largely neglected the Ego's vital role in determining how the archetypes will shape our everyday lives. With our model of the triangular structure of the archetypes, an individual can take care to see that the archetypes will manifest in their fullest form rather than in their Shadow structures. An Ego that does not properly *access* an archetype will be *possessed* by that archetype's Shadow, and left oscillating between the Shadow's two poles. At one the Ego will suffer *positive inflation* (explosion) and at the other *negative inflation* (implosion). Separated, the Shadow's two poles express a pathological darkness, which is only "enlightened" by polar integration into the transcendent third of the archetype. Their pathology is transformed by the Ego into a creative advance.

The action of the Ego is the key to this transformative experience. The Ego and the elements of the archetype exercise a kind of gravitational pull on each other. To allow transformation, the Ego must position itself "above" time and space, in the domain of the Spirit, or the collective unconscious. The Ego will serve ultimately as an occasion for the archetype's expression in time and space. Unless the Ego can work above the spatiotemporal dimension, the archetype will

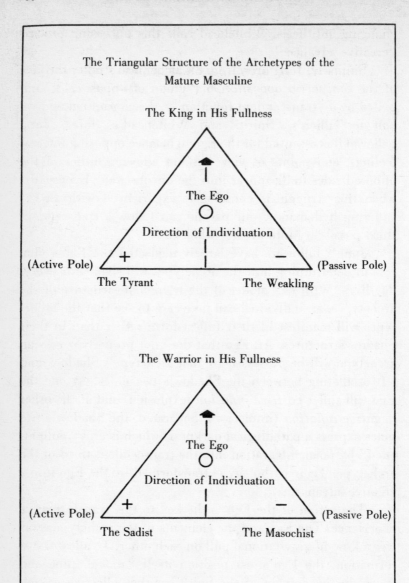

The Triangular Structure of the Archetypes of the
Mature Masculine

The King in His Fullness

The Ego

Direction of Individuation

(Active Pole)   (Passive Pole)

+   −

The Tyrant   The Weakling

The Warrior in His Fullness

The Ego

Direction of Individuation

(Active Pole)   (Passive Pole)

+   −

The Sadist   The Masochist

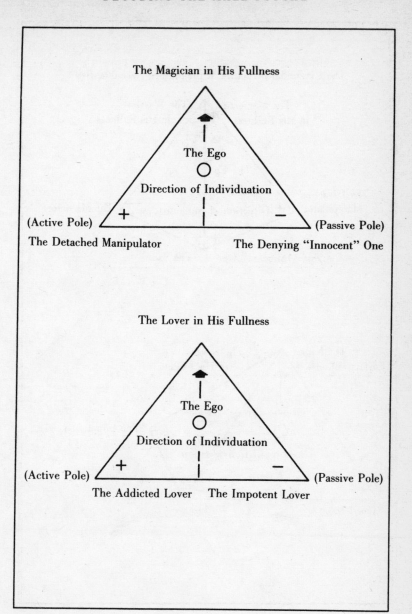

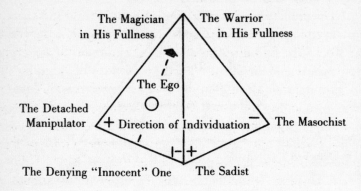

The Pyramidal Structure of the Mature Masculine Self

The Magician in His Fullness — The Warrior in His Fullness

The Ego

The Detached Manipulator + Direction of Individuation − The Masochist

The Denying "Innocent" One   The Sadist

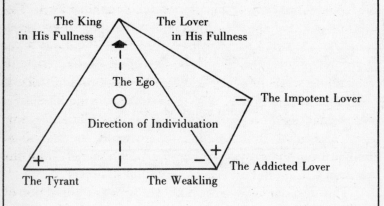

The King in His Fullness — The Lover in His Fullness

The Ego

Direction of Individuation

The Impotent Lover

The Tyrant   The Weakling   The Addicted Lover appear largely in its fragmented polar aspects, and the Ego will attract these to itself. In the Spirit's domain, the Ego can instead keep its proper fix on the lodestar the archetype's transcendent third represents.

The archetype's bipolar arrangement in time and space is portrayed in the mythic image of the Symplegades, the Clashing Rocks the Ego must pass between in pursuit of the archetype's transcendent third.[28] The Ego needs to be *lured* by this full expression of the archetype to experience creative advance on its own and in the world. And the archetype needs the Ego in order to experience itself in space and time, and to recover its lost Shadow fragments. The act of recovery empowers the archetype's ongoing creative action in the world.

According to our theory, there are four foundational archetypes of the mature masculine (as well as of the immature masculine). Each of these triangles—King, Warrior, Magician, and Lover—since they are interdependent aspects of the single masculine Self, fit together into a pyramidal form. The pyramid as it has appeared throughout the ages can be interpreted as a symbol for the masculine Self. Pyramids from Egypt to Mesoamerica, from Mesopotamia to Hawaii, are representations of the universe in miniature and often display a layered or stepped form. The layers of the pyramids nearly always stand for the layers of the universe, the different cosmic levels of reality. By ascending the pyramid, an individual climbed from the profane dimension to the sacred, from the less divine to the fullest manifestation of divinity.

This idea parallels ours about the "upward" direction of the Ego's individuation from a less integrated (profane) state to a fully integrated (sacred or "divine") state. A man's Ego must ascend the four faces of the stepped pyramid of the masculine Self, thereby overcoming the bipolar Shadow split at the base of each of the faces. The Ego must keep its eye on the capstone of the pyramid, which represents the fullest expression in an individual life of the four archetypes in perfect unity. This ascent of Ego-consciousness, according to Jung, is always a matter of reconciling opposites and of integrating split psychic materials. As a man's Ego ascends through each of the triangular structures of the archetypes, he becomes more integrated and whole. And he is better and better able to access the archetypes in their fullness at the top of the pyramid. On the King side, he integrates the Tyrant and the Weakling. On the Warrior face, he integrates the Sadist and the Masochist. On the Magician surface, he integrates the Detached Manipulator and the Denying "Innocent" One. And on the Lover side, he integrates the Addicted Lover with the Impotent Lover. Each of the poles of the split Shadows of the four major archetypes possesses insights and strengths that, when the Ego integrates them, contribute to a consolidated sense of Self. Each of the bipolar opposites, when united, reveals the "transcendent third" of the archetype in its fullness. By overcoming the splitness in the bipolar archetypal Shadows, a man comes to feel inwardly empowered. And, in a sense, while he is *building* internal masculine structure he is also *discovering* the pyramid of the masculine Self, which has always been within him, at his core.

THE ARCHETYPES AND BRAIN STRUCTURE

Startling resonances are being discovered between the fields of brain research and depth psychology. In his book *Archetypes: A Natural History of the Self*, the psychologist Anthony Stevens has extended the exploration of areas of the brain that may be the loci of archetypal forms.[29] He tries to explain Jung's theory of personality types in terms of brain structures. Jung's intuitive types, he speculates, might be using predominantly their Right Brains, and those who favor their Left

The "Mountain of God" at the Center of the Urban Complex
(The Temple Tower Esagila at Babylon: a reconstruction)

From Xibalba to the Skies
The Levels of Reality in the Maya Pyramid (Tikal)

Teotihuacán:

Raising the King-Energy and Generating a World

Stairway to the Sky:

Khmer Temple-Mountain of Koh Ker (tenth century A.D.)

Pyramid Power:
Great Morai Pappara, Otaheite (Tahiti)

The Masculine Self on a Monumental Scale:
The Pyramid of Khufu (Giza)

Brains would correspond to Jung's thinking types.

Briefly, the Right Brain (the right hemisphere of the cerebral cortex) "thinks" in images and symbols, grasps situations and patterns as wholes, and is the primary center for the generation of dreams, visions, and fantasies. The Left Brain (the corresponding left hemisphere) thinks sequentially, analyzes situations and patterns logically, and uses language in its cognitive processes. Many locate the Ego entirely in the Left Brain. In contrast, Stevens proposes that while the Ego may function most of the time in the Left Brain, it also draws on the Right Brain. Consciousness, he says, is a pervasive function of the whole brain, though Right- and Left-Brain modes of consciousness are quite distinct. The personal unconscious and its various complexes seem to manifest in the Right Brain. By dreaming, the Right Brain communicates with the still primarily Left Brain–identified Ego.

Rather than locating the archetypes in the Right Brain, Stevens proposes that they arise in deeper, older layers of the brain, layers that, according to brain researcher Paul MacLean, have remained largely unchanged for millions of years of animal evolution.[30] The dihemispheric cerebral cortex we think of as the human brain is only the most recently evolved element of three distinct neurological regions. Before it, in ascending order of antiquity, come the neocortex, or neomammalian brain, apparently responsible for cognition and sophisticated perception; the midbrain, or paleomammalian brain (limbic system), which seems to generate the basic emotions of fear and anger, affiliation, and maternity as well as species-characteristic individual and social behaviors; and the upward growth of the spinal cord, the reptilian brain, or R-complex, responsible for basic life activities, also probably the seat of our most basic instincts and our routine-driven behavior patterns. These three brains within a brain function relatively autonomously. Our process of psychological integration is, in part, an attempt to unify and synchronize these three regions of the brain.

If archetypes arise, as Jung believed, at a fundamentally instinctual level, then it could be that they originate in our most primitive region, the reptilian brain. Elaborated as they pass upward through the paleomammalian and neomammalian brains, the imagistic, intuitive structures of the archetypes would rise primarily into our Right Brains. But since our Ego's experience of the archetypes will also be mediated via the Left Brain, they will also be influenced by the linguistic and logical modes of thinking centered there. Archetypes hold a sense of otherness[31] perhaps because they originate in levels of the brain so much deeper than the source of Ego-consciousness, and then must be translated into terms that make sense especially to the Left Brain. Archetypes in their fullness involve *both* Left- and Right-Brain functions. This is clearly the case with the four foundational archetypes of the mature masculine, which we are outlining in this series. Certainly the rational, strategic, and emotionally detached modes of the Magician and the Warrior are characteristic of Left-Brain processes, although they seem to draw secondarily on Right-Brain functions, and the visually oriented, aesthetic, intuitive modes of the Lover are characteristic of Right-Brain functions, although the Lover also seems to draw on Left-Brain processes. We attempt a more thorough discussion of the origin of the four archetypes of mature masculinity and the brain's limbic system (paleomammalian brain) in Appendix B. This field of inquiry is wide open to exciting future research.

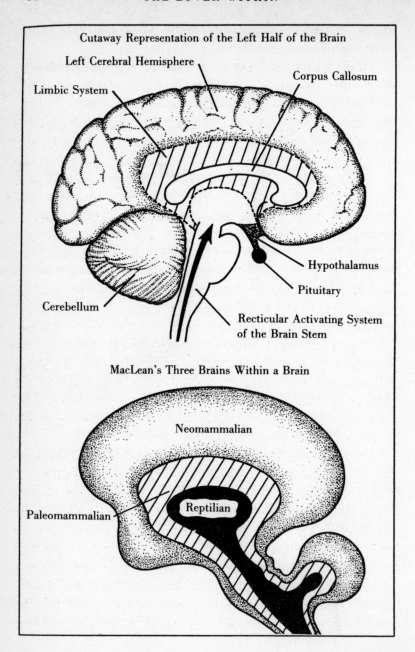

Cutaway Representation of the Left Half of the Brain

Left Cerebral Hemisphere

Limbic System

Corpus Callosum

Hypothalamus

Pituitary

Cerebellum

Recticular Activating System
of the Brain Stem

MacLean's Three Brains Within a Brain

Neomammalian

Paleomammalian

Reptilian

CONVERGENCE OF THE MATURE MASCULINE
ARCHETYPES

Depth psychologists often merge the mature masculine archetypes. Because only the most perfectly realized Ego apprehends an archetype's full expression, for most of us they
retain a degree of mystery. The very images and symbols
archetypes use to communicate to us refer beyond themselves
to other images and symbols in an almost infinitely complex
way. For example, the phallus, the cross, the tree, the *axis
mundi*, the spine, the sacred mountain, and the pyramid can
each be read symbolically as aspects of one another.[32] There
are dangers, however, involved with overinterpretations. An
individual can easily lose himself, as Yeats was warned in the
course of his occult researches, along the Path of the Chame-
leon, a labyrinthine trail of correspondences. Besides this, the
four basic archetypes that influence a mature man, the King,
the Warrior, the Magician, and the Lover, are the fragments of
a primevally whole Self, and complement each other to such
a degree that no one of them receives its fullest expression
without incorporating the others.

These archetypes have historically merged and diverged
again in a bewildering variety of configurations. Rain magicians, for example, give rise to rain kings, who appoint priests
to elect warrior kings, who commission other warriors to serve
magicians who themselves become kings. A mortal king, to
the extent that he fully expresses the archetypal King, is a
warrior who enforces order within his kingdom and who may
take military action to extend his kingdom. He is also a high-
priest magician who mediates between the spiritual dimension
and his people.[33] He is also a lover, of his people, and in a

special sense of his sacred queen, since he cannot rule legitimately or effectively unless their union is fruitful.[34] Despite
these uncertain boundaries, it is useful to distinguish masculine archetypes in order to enhance the Ego's capacity to
access these psychic structures in all their richness and complexity.

THE LOVER AND HIS PRIMATE PREFIGURATIONS

Chimpanzees are our closest living animal relatives.[35] Their
genetic profile is over 98 percent identical to ours.[36] Primate
ethology research suggests close correspondences between
their social structures and interpersonal behaviors and ours. It
seems likely that similar psychological processes are at work.[37]

While of course we cannot *know* fully what other animals
feel and think, in many ways we cannot be sure we *know* what
another *human* feels or thinks. In either case we make judg-
ments based on observable behaviors. Our great advantage in
observing humans obviously is spoken language, but we still
have the subjective task of interpreting linguistic signs. Chimpanzees, while they cannot speak, *can* communicate with us in
sign language and through other quasi-verbal methods designed by researchers.[38] In addition, their complex range of
body signals bears a striking resemblance to our own body
language. It seems reasonably safe to assume that when chimpanzees *appear* to be fearful, wrathful, submissive, loving, or
awed, they are in fact experiencing these emotions. Probably
their emotional experience is less self-conscious and complicated than ours, but still it offers clues into primate psychology, including our own.

The hierarchical power blocs and coalitions of chimpanzee society center around a dominant adult male ethologists
call the *Alpha Male*.[39] Successful Alpha Males are usually

King, Warrior, Magician, Lover:
The Alpha Male "Displaying" (Figan as Alpha Male at Gombe)

mature and physically powerful. They display foresight, courage, and what can only be called "character." Alpha Males
exhibit many behaviors common to the sacred king, the specific archetypally inspired figure we explored in *The King
Within.*

Alpha Males surround themselves with male "knights" to
help protect and defend their "realms." These warrior males
exhibit characteristics of what David Gilmore calls the "cult of
manhood" in human males. Like their human counterparts,
chimpanzee males are protectors and providers for the females
and the young of their societies.[40]

We believe the warrior males among chimpanzees, gorillas, and other primates are working out of archetypal structures similar to those of their human counterparts, albeit on
a much more primitive level. They defend their community
with great ferocity and at times pay for their efforts with their
lives.[41]

Human males experience this warrior role in a significantly more elaborate form. In one sense the gap between
other primates and the warriors of human history is an enormous one, millions of years long. In another sense, however,
the gap is small. It fits within our skulls! If Stevens and others
are right in their analysis of human brain structure, there is a
warrior male within us. We must learn to steward his energies
for the human community.

Alpha Males in chimpanzee and other primate societies
often show characteristics of the Magician function of the
human psyche. They frequently make decisions that call for
cognitive discernment—for example, when to move the troop
or the tribe in order to avoid predators, where best to camp for
the night, when it's time to change feeding sites, and so forth.
In addition, the Magician power, both as a function of modulating mechanisms in the primate brain that serve to balance
and control aggressive and sexual impulses, and as a function

Lovers in Paradise: Heart to Heart at Gombe

of higher thinking processes, is part of the psychological equipment of every chimpanzee—male and female—and is a hallmark of the primates in general. This creative, strategizing, reflective archetype enables chimpanzees in particular to make and use a wide range of tools—from clubs and stones to termite sticks and even "toilet paper"—strong evidence of incipient technology, one of the gifts of the Magician.

The archetypal male *Lover* appears in virtually all species of living things. And in our closest animal relatives, the common chimpanzees and the pygmy chimpanzees, or bonobos, he takes on humanlike form. Along with almost unceasing promiscuous sexual activity, especially among the bonobos, both chimpanzees and bonobos display what seems to be a prefiguration of human romantic love.

Primatologists have identified temporary monogamous pair-bonds between males and females that last anywhere from several days to a few weeks, and they call these romantic trysts "consortships." While these consortships last, the couples show all the signs of what we know as "falling in love." They gaze into each other's eyes, kiss, hold hands, and wander off into the forest to be alone together. When they return to the group the female is often pregnant. As someone once observed about our own species, romance seems to be nature's way of tricking us into intensified efforts to reproduce.

We offer this book and the series as a whole to the man who is looking for an operator's manual to the psyche, and to the woman who wants a guide to the hard wiring of men, and to her own inner masculine as well. Just as no jet pilot would try to fly a 747 without knowing its capabilities and instruments inside and out, the only way to "fly" successfully an immensely complicated male psyche is to know it inside and out, with a clear understanding of how to access its archetypal energy systems. The mindful use of this energy will bring a man safely into his mature manhood.

PART 2

IMAGES OF
THE MASCULINE
LOVER

3

THE GARDEN,
THE PHALLUS,
AND LIBIDO

WESTERN RELIGION HAS TRADITIONALLY BEEN deeply ambivalent about the Lover in the male psyche. For example, the Moslem culture has for fourteen centuries been a culture that often seems stern and life-denying. It urges upon its faithful a daily regimen of prayer, abstinence from alcohol and other drugs, and willing self-sacrifice on the battlefield. The Moslem religion is dominated by the Warrior and King archetypes.

Yet even in a religion that demands submission to a fierce, warlike Allah, the Lover has not been driven out of the collective unconscious. He reappeared in his characteristic

The Garden of Immortality: Phallus as the Tree of Life (Babylonian
cylinder seal, circa 1750–1550 B.C., Museum of The Hague)

Garden of Delight in the ecstatic visions of the Sufi mystics,
who experienced Allah as the gentle, life-giving Beloved, and
not the ascetic desert warrior of his more familiar aspect. This
Allah would call out to his mystics from every blade of grass
and grain of sand. Allah's self-sacrificing warriors longed now
for a perfumed garden teeming with birds, fountains, and
shady trees, where an eternal banquet was set for martyred
heroes, attended by dark-eyed houris who poured an unlimited supply of heavenly liquor.[1]

Along with their religious cousins the Moslems, Christians too have tried to banish the sensual and sexual forms of
the Lover from the unconscious. The Lover's sacred space, the
magical Garden, is deferred to the next life by both the Christian and the Islamic traditions. Christians are promised illimitable wealth in a New Jerusalem, where dazzling light shines on
the golden streets, and everyone's cup overflows with the
waters of life. God wipes away every tear there, and the cross
restores the ancient Tree of Life to world-weary peoples.[2]

In the Exile from the Garden, self-denial and asceticism

form the conscious ideal of our Western spiritual tradition. Christianity is deeply suspicious of the world, and enamored of disincarnation. Yet the Lover's life-bearing images and feelings appear in the Scripture, most clearly, perhaps, in the Song of Solomon. Medieval mystics once again attended his call, as did the "heretical" troubadours. And finally whole cultures, inspired by the Lover, burst into the spectacular flowering of the Renaissance.

Our schizophrenic modern culture has a painfully ambivalent relationship with the Lover. We tend to accelerate a divorce from the Lover through a misdirected ascetic spirituality, which takes us out of the realm of instinctual pleasure. On the other hand, we tend to approve of those who rush into the Lover's sacred space like "fools," though the Garden is a place "where angels fear to tread."

The Garden of Delight is the archetypal image of the Lover's sacred space. Within it can be found the Tree of Life flourishing by the Waters of Life,[3] the lion and the lamb lying down together,[4] Kaikobad and Jamshyd dallying,[5] Krishna dancing his eternal dance of love with the gopis,[6] and Adam and Eve playing in the eternity they share before tasting the forbidden fruit.[7]

The Garden of Delight figures in ancient Sumerian and Babylonian cylinder seals. These seals were used to impress, on strips of clay, demons, angels, and miniature wonderlands of dream animals, magic mountains, fairyland trees, and enchanted streams. Central to these glimpses over the "wall" that separates our mundane world from Paradise is the Tree of Life. Often it is flanked by cherubim—fantastic gatekeepers whose images are generated by the deep unconscious. They guard the phallus of the Lover, from which springs every man's most secret and central joy.

Ancient Evenings, Norman Mailer's fictional exploration of Egyptian palace life, weaves the spell of the Lover in all his "polymorphous perversity." The great harem of Rameses II is central to Mailer's lavish and sensuous novel. Hermetically sealed from the outside world by a retaining wall, and manned by an army of eunuchs, the royal harem is designed to make the pharaoh immortal through unlimited sexual pleasure. Within its magical confines myrrh and cedar-scented lanes wind through beds of exotic flowers, beneath trees brought from all corners of the known world, and beyond lily-dappled fish ponds, up to the doorways of the royal concubines. Past their lintels beautiful women of every race, form, and description are trained in the most fantastic techniques of lovemaking. Within the harem time stands still, and past moments of indescribable pleasure seem to hang in the air like perfume. To enter the harem is to enter an idyllic life beyond the tomb.

The ancient Egyptians were the first people we know of to write love songs.[8] Our own love songs are heir to millennia of such songs, the lyrics and melodies inspired by the erotic, heavenly "music of the spheres," which wafts over the Wall of Paradise to us. The human voice tries to embody for the ear and the heart a lost but uncannily familiar wonderland.

By his own admission Cardinal Nicholas of Cusa, a fifteenth-century Christian mystic and theologian, regularly drew close to the Wall within the depths of his own soul. Climbing a tree he found just outside of it, he looked over the top to the dazzling wonders on the other side. He constructed an entire theology around the indescribable beauty and mystery he saw in his excursions. His "Wall of Paradise" played a central role, dividing *this* world of time and space from *that* one of bliss and harmony. He knew that the key to Paradise is love. And he taught that intellectual and emotional acceptance of the paradoxical nature of love is the only way human beings can venture into the Lover's sacred space.

Like every mystic before and after him—whether Moslem or Taoist or Hindu—Cusa saw that beyond the Wall of

Paradise love brings opposites into a complex unity. His Wall is a typical image of the boundary between the eternal, infinite One, and its expression in creation first as the Two, and then the Manifold. On our side of the boundary opposites appear to be irreconcilable. Yet once we learn of love's mysteries, we recognize that though we are all of us individual, finite beings, at the same time, on the deepest level, we are all One, pure and undivided.[9]

In fact once we enter the Garden of Delight we experience the full ecstasy of being ourselves just at the time we feel most at one with others. It is at the boundary of the Lover's sacred space that Osiris and Set, the ancient Egyptian Gods of death and life, clasp hands in their paradoxical, eternal union.[10] It is at this boundary that Christ "swallows up" death, in St. Paul's words, and as he ingests it, transforms it for the purposes of eternal life.[11] Modern physics and cosmology teach us of a similar union of opposites in the subatomic realm, and in the immeasurably brief Planck Era that immediately preceded the Big Bang.[12] Depth psychologists know that only when an individual can embrace his Shadow will he enter into the blissful condition of being at one with himself.[13] As he returns to the Garden, he must accept other aspects of his psyche as well, including his Anima and the eternal Child that dwells at his center.[14]

In the old song "Toyland" we are told that we cannot go back to the world of childhood once we have passed "its portals." And yet, Jesus holds that we *can* return, if we "become as little children" and are "born again."[15] Then we can enter the Kingdom of Heaven—another name for the Garden of Delight.

Despite the nostalgic grief of the song, we do unconsciously try to follow Jesus' injunction, and return to the sacred space we knew as children. But instead of returning to the ecstasy that typifies the core of the child's world, we end up recapturing the superficial dimensions of our own, personal childhood experiences. We endow places such as New Orleans at Mardi Gras time, Disney World, Las Vegas, Rio de Janeiro, and other "magical" locations with the liminal qualities of the Lover's sacred space. As a consequence we look forward to spending recreational time in these places—and in so doing we "recreate" the Garden for ourselves. In such places we celebrate what Freud called the "polymorphous perversities"[16] of our eternal Child.

In many of these places, an attempt has been made to integrate these Shadow urges into the culture. A city like New Orleans becomes a desirable place for a vacation because of the Mardi Gras atmosphere it offers. When in New Orleans we feel we can "give the Devil his due." Mardi Gras is a ritualized period of time within which all our "perverse" energies can be displayed and honored. The feeling of most participants is that nobody needs to be ashamed about what he does during Mardi Gras.

New Orleans inhabitants might like us to believe that Mardi Gras is a Cajun tradition, not to be found outside their city. But the carnivals and festivals of Brazil and Europe give the lie to that idea. Jung was fascinated by *Fastnacht,* the carnival celebrated in his native Switzerland.[17] He noted how the proceedings were colored by ritualization. A long historical tradition in Basel, his birthplace, kept the energies of *Fastnacht* channeled into a delightful social release. By contrast, in Zurich, the metropolitan city where he worked, the everyday lack of social fabric and order meant that the ritualized breakdown of order had sometimes an unpleasant and antisocial edge.

These energies are ritualized in many arenas within our own culture. Anyone who has been in New York or Chicago on St. Patrick's Day has witnessed what is essentially a disorganized carnival. As time goes on these fairly impromptu celebrations may be as (relatively) focused as is the Mardi Gras. Rock concerts also aim to, and sometimes succeed in, channeling our Lover energies. The office Christmas party is another ubiquitous ritual means of invoking the Lover, and of entering (however superficially) into the Garden of Delight.

THE PHALLUS

The King's sacred space is the city, which is by extension the kingdom, or cosmos. The sacred space of the Warrior is the field of combat, or Armageddon. The Magician has his sacred magic circle, and the Lover his garden. These are all images of the spaces within the center of the masculine psyche, as it brings creative order to itself and the world around it.

There are also similarities between the power emblems of the different masculine archetypes—the King's scepter, the Warrior's sword, and the Magician's wand. Ultimately these specialized expressions of archetypal masculine energy are all manifestations of the Lover's phallus.

In a physical and literal sense, the phallus is the fully engorged penis. In a spiritual sense a phallus is more than a penis. It is the archaic, instinctual Libido which drives a man's enthusiasms, and his spirituality too. According to the para-doxical nature of the Lover, though these forms are distinct, they share the same ultimate goal.

Everywhere we look we can see the underlying presence of phallic rejoicing. Just as theologians once found the signa-ture of Christ imprinted on all the things of this world, we see the Lover's phallus in the forms of nature, in crystal spires, in volcanic eruptions, rocket launches, and the artistic and ar-chitectural works of humankind. Hindu temples rise from the dusty plains of India like enormous, tatooed organs. Mayan pyramids lift to the sky from out of the verdant jungle, and

Mamallapuram: Shrine with Lingam
(central shrine of the Trimurti cave,
India, seventh century)

modern skyscrapers soar into the heavens, proclaiming our
phallic magnificence. These creations of masculine life-force
leave little doubt that the fully engorged phallus inspires the
imaginal forms which artists and architects, engineers and
scientists incarnate on canvas and in stone, or in the death-
defying pyrotechnics of space flight.

These and other joyful expressions of phallic masculine
creativity are often ridiculed and shamed today in the polar-
ized climate of contemporary gender politics. We must not let
such sexist depreciations of phallus obscure our awareness of
and appreciation for these authentic manifestations of the
male soul.

In the mythologies of our species, masculine phallic energy has been embodied in a number of divine beings. The
Hindus' cosmic king, Shiva, generates the world by means of
his mighty *lingam*, which simultaneously arises from and
penetrates the *yoni* of the Great Mother.[18] It is so high that
although other Gods have tried to follow its length into the

heavens, they have never yet reached the top of it. And it is so deep that none have ever found its source. All the Gods can do, when confronted with Shiva's giant phallus, is travel up and down along it. Quite a contrast to the often effeminate, and usually asexual, images of Christ *our* culture has produced.

The Roman God of the phallus, Priapus, walks about with a huge, continuous, erection. In many of the images of him discovered in the excavations of ancient Pompeii, he has taken human form, holding his oversized penis for all to see and be inspired by. Sometimes he is represented merely by a swollen penis, painted red to dramatize his potency. Wall paintings of Geb, the Earth God of the ancient Egyptians, show him thrusting his huge penis skyward. He is in the midst of ecstatic union with Nut, Goddess of the Heavens; he is impregnating her, thereby engendering the other Gods and all the rest of the created world.

On ancient Greek pottery, Dionysus, the God of phallic ecstasy, everywhere appears swinging his ivy-wrapped *thyrsos*, a magic staff, and brandishing a huge goblet of wine. A smile teases up the corners of his mouth. His frenzied female worshipers, the maenads, and the leaping satyrs with fully erect penises accompany him.

Dionysus is clearly an example of masculine beauty—in his images he is represented like the handsome dark-haired, olive-skinned youths one can still see in the bars and on the beaches of Athens. Yet certain of his features are not to be found on a young man. He has a long beard, which gives him a mature appearance. He wears his hair long and free, flowing down the middle of his back. To the ancient Greeks, who abhorred long hair on men, this gave him a distinctly feminine appearance. Dionysus also wears a woman's dress. The vine and the staff he carries are symbols of his life-giving phallus. Like Mick Jagger and so many contemporary performers,

Dionysus Enraptured: A State of Ecstasy (from an ancient Greek
ceramic piece)

Dionysus cultivates both his masculine and his feminine qualities.

Mythically Dionysus, like Christ, was a God-man. Indeed Christ owes many of his archetypal characteristics to
Dionysus, and many Greek Easter rituals are taken directly
from Dionysian celebrations. Dionysus was the offspring of
Zeus and a mortal woman, Semele. Like Christ after him,
Dionysus was a savior God who died and was then resurrected.
His enemies—the enemies of love and joy and ecstasy—per-
secuted and imprisoned him. And like Christ, Dionysus burst
the bonds of imprisonment, rising triumphantly to lead his
followers back to the Garden of Delight.

The God of sensuality and pleasure, Dionysus was also

the Deity of spiritual ecstasy and flights of the soul. His worshipers were offered an immediate, direct experience of the
reality behind appearances. Like Christ, he was the bearer of
wisdom and of "the peace which passes understanding." His
dress and his behavior signified the union of masculine and
feminine impulses. His orgies were enactments of a primordial, instinctual urge for the union of opposites. He was the
God of life and death, and of the transfiguration of death *into*
life. As the reconciler of opposites, he was the means for his
worshipers to find their way back to the other side of the Wall
of Paradise.

To see him merely as "the god of wine" is to completely
miss the point of his power. Dionysus led his followers to the
gateway of the vast world of the unconscious, and to the Self
beyond the Wall. Hence he was the God of theater, of tragedy,
and of *eukatastrophe*, or joyous, sudden turning.

One Dionysian myth tells of his capture by a group of
pirates.[19] They take him aboard their vessel, bind him to the
mast, and set sail. Dionysus warns them to let him go. When
they refuse, the God bursts his bonds, and transforms the
ship. The mast becomes a giant grape vine, whose tendrils and
fragrant clusters race along the deck and entangle the oars.
One helmsman offers obeisance to Dionysus, and is spared—
but all the other pirates are cast overboard and turned into
dolphins, who leap and play in the waters around the ship.

The myth can be read as a warning. Masculine life-force,
when enriched both by the Shadow and by "feminine" gentle-
ness, is irrepressible. Any attempts to "bind" or repress it are
doomed to failure. It will burst forth and transform the psyche
(represented by the vessel in the story) in spite of the repressive efforts of the Ego (the pirate crew). The Lover will cast the
Ego back into the unconscious (the sea) before he will brook
the Ego's denial of Libido.

The phallus that often appears in the dreams of modern

Western men, sometimes in the person of Dionysus, works to reorient their lives in life-affirming and generative ways. One middle-aged analysand was feeling sexually repressed, and was experiencing life as "all work and no play." Because he had lost touch with his youthful enthusiasm and zest for life, he had the following dream:

> I was lost in a kind of desert. I felt sick, cut off from life. It was not a sunlit desert though. That would have been at least a little cheerful. Rather, it was a dark desert. The sand and the sky were brown and black, and everything was kind of soupy, almost like a sea of shit. I was thrashing around in this dark desert soup, when from down below me a huge dark brown snake rose up, a very fat snake, and started pushing upward to where I was. As it came by me on its way up—wherever up was—I grabbed a hold of it, put my arms and legs around it, and rode it. I felt powerful and primitive. And in an impersonal way, the "snake" felt benevolent and good. I could see myself from outside of myself, holding onto this giant "snake," which now took the clear form of a great phallus. I rode this phallus into the light.

The archetypal phallus of the Lover, rising from the darkness of the body and of instinct, cthonic (or "earthly") and underground, carried the dreamer's Ego up out of his depression and toward a spiritual realm of light and joy.

Psychologists have long distinguished Dionysian from Apollonian personality types. The Dionysian man is held to be more intuitive, artistic, in touch with his feelings, and inclined to be motivated by pleasure than the Apollonian. All of these characteristics are typically described as being more "feminine." The Apollonian man is supposed to be more hard-headed, practical, rational, and "masculine." We would characterize him as acting under the influence primarily of the

King and the Warrior, where the Dionysian man is more influenced by the Lover.

Jean Bolen has tried to demonstrate how ancient Greek Gods correspond to the personality types of actual men.[20] Much of her work is insightful, as the Greek myths are usefully interpreted as parables of personality interactions. The best of the ancient Greek dramatists did the same useful work, and their plays survive because of their continued psychological resonance. Bolen is mistaken, however, when she claims that the Gods are archetypes, because they are really a culture-specific mix of the more basic King, Warrior, Magician, and Lover structures. Every God has a developed personality, whereas archetypes do not—they are subhuman structures. Bolen singles Dionysus out as the primary carrier of the masculine Shadow, whereas in fact every God, and each of the archetypes underlying the Gods, has its own specific Shadow system. Bolen also seems to equate Dionysus with the Lover. While Dionysus embodies the Lover, he also draws on King, Warrior, and Magician structures. Other Gods, such as Zeus, draw on the Lover, despite the primary influence of one masculine archetype or another. Any personality may tend to be influenced mostly by one archetype, and it is certainly true that Dionysus is closer than the other Gods to the Lover's passionate fires. But in another culture the Lover may be embodied in quite a different God-image, with a dissimilar personality.

LIBIDO

Every school of psychology differs in its definition of Libido. Some believe it to be a neutral force, neither inherently creative nor destructive. Others characterize this life-force as being held in a state of dynamic tension between the "life instinct" and the "death instinct." Some believe Libido should be identified with the positive impulse toward life, and so they call the counter force "anti-libidinal ego."

We believe that Libido is the profound and complex expression of love and the Lover. The life-force that energizes the archetype of the Lover cannot simply be defined as sexual energy, contrary to the views of the classical Freudians. Nor is the Lover energy a simple matter of life and death instincts—in an eerie way Libido strives, simultaneously, toward both life and death. While profoundly earthy, sensual, and sexual, and while pressed into the service of procreation, Libido also aims at a spiritual condition which can be described as "cosmic consciousness." Libido is at once a drive toward multiplicity—through discrete, finite entities which affirm, protect, and extend their boundaries—and an impulse toward the union of entities.

This two-fold drive of Libido has been elaborated from ancient times to the present in various forms of process philosophy. Process philosophies are those which show a deep appreciation for a dynamic program of cosmic development in space and time. Hegel, the early nineteenth-century German philosopher, proposed the famous formula "thesis, antithesis, synthesis" to describe the process of nature. Thesis is a first manifestation of unity. Antithesis is the opposite impulse toward differentiation and multiplicity. Thesis and antithesis are finally drawn together into a union, the synthesis, which is more complex than the original union, and which represents a generative advance. A later process philosopher, Alfred North Whitehead, constructed his creative philosophy around dynamic processes. He believed that he could see a creative advance unfolding in each "temporal occasion" of the finite world.

Paul Tillich, the great twentieth-century theologian, employed a similar notion of process. In his system, the world of time and space is characterized by a structure of *ambiguity*, of opposites in tension. Ambiguities are transcended by the power of the "Spirit," and lifted "above" time into "eternity." This sacred place above time is, we believe, the Garden of Delight, and the Spirit which resolves the ambiguities is the Lover.

Jung described a similar synthetic process of differentiation in the psyche that leads ultimately to a richer state of integration. He called this process *individuation*, and the driving force of this movement toward individual and collective integration he called the "transcendent function."

The human psyche is organized according to a similar dynamic process. Its essential building blocks are archetypal structures. These separate structures are integrated at the deepest levels of the psyche (in the "inner" Garden), but they fracture as they encounter the fragmenting effects of life. It is the Lover energy that urges us to rediscover the lost unity of the archetypes. The Lover remembers the original unity of the psyche, and throughout the course of our lives, drives us toward the recovery of that unity in complex form.

Within the Self, at the center of the psyche—just as in Nicholas of Cusa's Paradise—all ambiguities are reconciled. They are divergent without being in opposition. Within the Self, each of the Anima, the Shadow, the various neuroses and complexes, and the archetypes thrive in a dynamic quiescence which resolves into a whole. The Self draws the fragments of our psyches together with the power of love.

THE GOALS OF THE LOVER

All of us are wounded lovers. We have all sustained emotional injuries that have been far more devastating than we like to admit. Deep wounding in our period of "primary narcissism"

Friendship Love: Men Risking Their Lives for Other Men (Vietnam)

makes it exceedingly difficult for us to access the archetypes
of masculine maturity in appropriately life-enhancing ways.[21]
And what is true for our relationship with the other three
archetypes of mature masculinity is perhaps most true of our
relationship with the Lover. Love from our primary caregiv-
ers, usually our parents, is the key to psychological well-being
later in life. The lack of sufficient love (from "good-enough"
parents who supported us and celebrated us adequately) is the
major cause of our problems in adult life.

   We can interpret the developmental psychologist Alice
Miller's brilliant insights into the nature of early childhood
wounding in terms of the damage done to our connection with
the archetypal Lover. In Miller's treatment system, the griev-
ing that we must do involves the emotional, as well as cognitive, recognition that the love we needed, in the way in which
we needed it, will never be ours. We can never experience this
love fully in the context of our human relationships.

Harville Hendrix, in his popular book *Getting the Love You Want*, takes a somewhat different approach to the goal of the Lover. Hendrix argues that we can get the love we missed when we were children, if we can develop a "conscious marriage," an intimate relationship with a person who seems to have exactly the same negative, love-withholding characteristics of our parents. He claims, though he uses the term "Child" instead of "Lover," that the goal of the Lover is to repeat the relationship patterns of childhood with a person who matches the inner Child's Imago of the parents. The man who repeats his childhood does so in order to be healed, and to expand his own capacity to love himself and others. Ideally, he will achieve this reunion at the same time that he affirms his own individuality, and his own boundaries.

In addition to working through issues involving the Imago, Hendrix believes that the Child within also seeks, through loving a person of the opposite sex, to recover lost elements of his True Self. Those lost elements include what Hendrix calls the "Lost Self" and the "Disowned Self." Miller and Hendrix alike seem to be saying that the longing of the Lover is to recover the love of the parents. Miller emphasizes the impossibility of this project, as long as the project is designed and manipulated by the inner Child. Hendrix, in contrast, believes that this problematic project is indeed capable of successful resolution.

Norman O. Brown, the Freudian philosopher, in his *Life Against Death* and *Love's Body* has drawn out some implications of Freud's thought about the life instinct and eros. Brown believes that the goal of love, no matter how defended against and how sublimated by cultural imperatives, is to return to the situation of the child at the mother's breast. For Brown, the acceptance of the primacy of the "pleasure principle" forces us to the realization that all culture, and all thinking and reflecting, are, ultimately, neurotic. What the Child within strives to attain is a lost paradise of symbiotic union with a nurturing and life-giving mother.

Don Browning has pointed out that Brown is really saying the goal of eros is permanent regression to an eternity of infantilism. This would be a state of unconscious merger with the mother. From here no forward movement, no generativity would be possible. Browning asks, "Why stop with the situation of the infant at the mother's breast? Why not regress all the way to the condition of even more perfect merger, that of the fetus in the womb?"[22] For that matter, why not regress the fetus beyond the vanishing point to before it was a fetus at all, before it even existed as a finite entity in any sense?

If the goal of the Lover is complete regression to a paradise before the birth of individual consciousness—or even before the birth of an individual being—then could we not say that the goal of the Lover is death?

Another Freudian philosopher, Herbert Marcuse, in *Eros and Civilization*, takes up this question. Marcuse follows Freud's speculations on the interrelationship between the life and death instincts (eros and thanatos). Like Brown, Marcuse elaborates what he regards as the logical conclusions of Freud's ideas. Marcuse believes that eros and thanatos are originally at one in the Child. At an early developmental stage, they diverge into opposite drives, the one affirming life, the other destroying it. The death instinct, according to Marcuse, is the "Nirvana principle," an impulse within the human psyche to return to the condition of inorganic existence.[23]

One way in which we can envision the Lover aiming at both life and death is to experience, with Nicholas of Cusa, the paradoxical union of opposites beyond the Wall of Paradise in the primordial Self. On one level, the death instinct is the affirmation of the finite psyche's own boundaries. It is, as Marcuse says, the psyche's capacity to say "No"—in other words, to say, "No, I am not that." This negating of the other,

as a part of the organism's process of self-definition, is an
expression of the death instinct. As Marcuse points out, this
negation, though perhaps necessary, can turn destructive
when it is acted out.

The death instinct manifests as that very drive for merger
with the All which, for the mystics, expresses itself in feelings
of ecstasy and the vivid transcendence of individual life and
Ego-consciousness. In this case, the death instinct does not
negate the other, but rather cries out to the other with a
cosmic "Yes." Contrary to Freudian understandings, what the
Buddha had in mind with his concept of Nirvana was not a
drastic regression to unconsciousness, but rather a state of
higher *consciousness* in which the Ego is transcended and the
"Essence of Mind" is embraced. This is surely not death in
any usual sense, but greatly intensified life.[24]

The Lover energy urges us toward life and "death"
simultaneously. The Lover seeks to reconcile these and all
other opposites, in a paradoxically differentiated and integrated Self.

En route to the sacred psychological and spiritual space
of the Lover is what Bernard Meland has called, rather con-
servatively, "appreciative consciousness." Appreciative consciousness is the sensitive awareness of the inherent value of
all things. It is akin to the mystical ability "To see a World in
a Grain of Sand."[25] And it opens the mind and the heart to the
possibility of that paradoxical death in life that the Lover
urges us toward.

ASPECTS OF THE LOVER

There are many forms of love. The Greeks classified at least
four kinds: *eros, storge, philia,* and *agape.*[26] *Eros* is the form
we most often think of when we think of love—because it is

In the Garden: Krishna and Radha Embracing
(Kangra painting, India, late eighteenth century)

the form addressed by love songs and poems, and romantic
movies and novels.

Besides eros, there is the love of parents for children, of
children for parents, and of siblings and cousins for one another. The ancient Greeks called these forms of affection
storge.

Friends of the same or opposite sex share a third form of
love, which the ancient Greeks called *philia*. Again the sexual
dimension is downplayed in the pure form of philia. Intimacy
is important, even essential to this form of love; through the
sharing of intimate perceptions and feelings two friends come
to care for each other, and regard one another as equals.

Agape is the term used by the ancient Greeks to refer to
"fellow feeling." In agape, the Ego becomes merged with the
other. It is an unconditional and selfless love for humanity that

many mystics and philosophers describe as divine.

Each form of love possesses a slightly different feeling tone. Often, one form of love shades imperceptibly into another, or several forms are mixed together. Several of the forms can, in fact, be identified with the foundational archetypes. When the Lover predominates, eros is his primary expression. But when the King energy is dominant in a personality, and the Lover is present as well, that individual tends to value agape most. Warrior lovers experience philia for one another, as comrades-in-arms. There are many men who have known love most intensely in that dimension. Sports fans know this form of love as well, albeit vicariously. We shall examine later what happens when the Lover is absent from a King or Warrior personality.

The Magician-dominated personality, because of its essential detachment, has the hardest time making contact with the Lover. When there is no connection, the Lover's urges are expressed through *necrophilia*, the love of death. The necrophiliac is the armaments scientist developing ever-more effective ways to destroy others. He is the clever entrepreneur seeking to turn a profit through the deforestation of the planet.

Many commentators on the phenomenon of love telescope the many forms of this most complex of human emotions into only two, eros and agape. As a consequence, these two conceptualizations have been pushed and pulled completely out of shape. The Freudians use *eros* to refer to our sexual instinct primarily. Jungians, like the Freudians, tend to use the term *eros* in this more restricted sense as well, but they also use it in the more general sense found in the ancient Greek philosophical tradition. Some scholars represent eros and agape as being mutually antagonistic. To them agape is "self-sacrificial," whereas eros is "acquisitive."

But even within a narrow definition of erotic love, at the

point of ecstasy eros clearly becomes self-sacrificial. The Ego gives itself over to a state of mind and of soul that transcends the Ego's interests. We say we can "die of love," and that we would gladly do so for the sake of our beloved. Agape is often presented as "selfless" or "other-directed" love, whereas eros is disparaged as a form of love that is "selfish" or "self-directed." And yet, in the New Testament—the primary literary source for our understanding of agape—Jesus makes it clear that one of the most important reasons for us to come to feel agape for others is so that we can realize our "reward in heaven," and gain our own personal resurrection.[27] These are unquestionably self-fulfilling goals.

EROS

The ancient Greek philosophers Parmenides and Empedocles theorized that eros was the "cosmic power of harmony and life."[28] Boethius believed that eros held earth, sea, and sky in place, as well as society, marriage, and friendship.[29] To his mind, eros was a kind of universal glue cementing together diverse elements in nature and in the human psyche.

The doctrine of eros is most fully developed by Plato. According to Plato, eros is the yearning of the human soul for union with the Divine.[30] Humankind's essence is spiritual and belongs to the world of light beyond time and space. Led by eros, we experience *anamnesis*; we remember what we beheld and knew in the eternal world before we fell into our fragmented, and fragmenting, world. Eros begins when the soul, stimulated by sensuous or sexual pleasure, desires union with the remembered beauties of the Garden of Delight. The soul gradually rises heavenward as it comes to realize that the union it longs for cannot be attained in this world. Thus eros, originally sensual and sexual in nature, becomes a profoundly

The Eros

"Everything that Rises must Converge"

Avalokiteśvara: Bodhisattvas and
Universal Love (Ajantā, India)

spiritualizing drive. The experience of eros becomes a means
of salvation for the soul. This salvation is achieved through
ecstasy. The ecstatic Ego loses itself in the terrible joy of
passionate union, which ultimately implies a union with God.

Philo of Alexandria, the great Jewish scholar (30 B.C.–
A.D. 40), translated the central command of Judaism—to love
God with all one's heart, and mind, and strength—not with
the word *agape*, but with *eros*.[31] Plotinus passed a heavily
intellectualized version of this erotic idea on to Christian theologians and mystics.[32] Throughout the Middle Ages, Christian
mystics like St. Teresa and St. Bernard, and the Moslem Sufi
mystics, among them Ibn al-Farìd, Rùmì, and Ibn'Arab ì,
often spoke of their passion for God in frankly erotic language.[33]

Eros values the finite entities of the material world, although it drives the psyche "upward" toward final union with an immortal and infinite spiritual reality. From a Freudian point of view, spiritualized eros is "sublimated infantile sexuality."[34] This Freudian reduction of the spiritual impulse to neurotic repression and the sublimation of simple sexuality seems to Jungians to be inaccurate and overly narrow in its conception of the life-force. For Jungians, sensually and sexually focused eros and spiritualized eros are divergent, yet they are ultimately one impulse—the paradoxical impulse toward union *in* diversity.

Both aspects of eros drive the psyche toward vivid and passionate experience. The one drives the psyche "downward" to its archaic roots, and values the instincts from which human consciousness and human being arise. The other drives the psyche "upward" into realms that transcend individual Ego-consciousness, and perhaps even the biological foundations of the organism. The Jungian vision of wholeness affirms that both body and soul are indispensable for fullness of being. It affirms that what it calls the "sensation function" (materially directed eros) and the "thinking function" (eros that is cognitively directed), as well as the other major functions of the whole human being, need to be integrated into a rich and complex unity.[35]

AGAPE

When the New Testament says that "God is Love," the Greek term used is *agape*.[36] St. Paul is the primary source for the current Western conception of agape. His famous "Hymn to Love" (I Cor. 13) provides essential insights into his idea of agapetic love:

> If I speak in the tongues of men and of angels, but have not love, I am a noisy gong or a clanging cymbal. And if

I have prophetic powers, and understand all mysteries and all knowledge, and if I have all faith, so as to remove mountains, but have not love, I am nothing. . . . Love is patient and kind; love is not jealous or boastful; it is not arrogant or rude. Love does not insist on its own way; it is not irritable or resentful; it does not rejoice at wrong, but rejoices in the right. Love bears all things, believes all things, hopes all things, endures all things.

Love never ends. . . .

Throughout the centuries, Christian apologists have wrestled with the question of the relationship between eros and agape. Some writers, such as the Scandinavian theologian Anders Nygren, have seen these two forms of Lover energy as engaged in a "life and death struggle" with each other.[37] Nygren insists that agape is not a sublimated expression of infantile sexuality. He claims that agape is something entirely different, something disconnected from natural human being. He believes that while eros may arise from our biological roots of flesh and blood, agape has its origin in God. He sees God as being completely outside the realm of the human psyche. This is, from a Jungian perspective, a psychologically naïve position. The image of God, or the "God-concept," is clearly within the psyche, since it is an embodied experience of a psychological reality.

Nygren sees agape as spontaneous, unmotivated, indifferent to value, creative, unlimited, unconditioned, and uncalculating. He contrasts this with the qualities of eros. Eros bases its interest in a single other, instead of all others; eros is hence limited, conditioned, and preeminently calculating. Agape, says Nygren, "is a love that gives itself away, that sacrifices itself, even to the uttermost."[38] And yet *agape*, in normal ancient Greek usage, had a number of meanings, including "to long for," "to prefer," or "to prize"[39]—all qualities that stand opposed to Nygren's definition of agape, and all of which sound more like his pejorative charges against eros.

The popular understanding of the contrast between these two forms of Lover energy seems far more accurate. Eros is sensual and sexual in its origins. It never loses its connection to the body and to the material world of space and time no matter how spiritualized or sublimated it becomes. Agape, like eros, arises in the human psyche. Ironically it is what we understand by the phrase "Platonic love." Agape is just as self-serving and self-transcending as eros, but it lacks the element of sensual and sexual passion.

The forms of agape are many. Most love relationships are characterized more by agape than they are by eros, although elements of eros are present to some extent in nearly all such relationships. Even if agape is the love of "everyone in particular,"[40] or the love of the neighbor "in his concrete situation and his concrete condition, not some imagined ideal of my neighbor and not God in my neighbor," the passionate appreciation of everyone certainly has erotic overtones.[41] The love that loves all things equally, without valuing and without selection, is surely that same spiritualized *eros* by which the mystics of every spiritual tradition have aspired to attaining a state of cosmic consciousness. In the end, the sensual, even sexual experience of others leads toward ecstatic, spiritualized union.

From our point of view, eros and agape, however distinct they may be on one level, are ultimately the same Lover energy. The two terms have unfortunately been so loaded with differing and propagandistic meanings that they have become more confusing than enlightening. Joseph Campbell has suggested a way of resolving the conflict between these two forms of love, and between their respective proponents.[42]

The Cult of Romantic Love (page from the
Manesse Codex, Troubadour Werner von Teufen)

AMOR

Often Christians, following the New Testament hostility toward the world of the flesh, have first tried to reduce eros to
lust, and then tried to banish lust from the human psyche. St.
Paul used Christ as a symbol for the Lover, saying that he was
"neither male nor female."[43] Such language reflects a profoundly asexual, even antisexual, bias in the agapetic Christian
view of love. Modern secular culture, fed up with pleasureless
spiritual abstractions, has revolted against Christian repression; we have elevated the material world and the world of the
senses, and depreciated the *Spirit*. The modern Western world
prefers the Lover in his Dionysian, or erotic, aspect. A third
way of considering love may be seen in Campbell's formula-

tion of love as *amor*. Amor is, in effect, a merger of the two most common Western expressions of love.

Amor is at once sexual and spiritual, both incarnated and transcendent. It is the love of spirit for spirit and of flesh for flesh, spirit for flesh and flesh for spirit. It is the "passionate (erotic) friendship (agapetic)"[44] of one human being for another. It involves experiencing the "lost paradise" within the psyche, between the masculine and feminine elements in every man and in every woman.

Campbell relates amor to *minne*, the Germanic word for ecstatic love between the sexes. He talks about the celebration of amor in Western cultures as it appears in the cult of romantic love, which the troubadours and minnesingers exalted as the highest expression of love. While for them, amor was *dis*incarnate to the extent that it was not to be realized in actual physical union, it was *in*carnate in the sense that the object of the lover's passion was a mortal woman rather than the Blessed Virgin.

Amor has continued to develop in our culture beyond the troubadour tradition. The mortal lover, much like a Platonic philosopher or religious mystic, experiences the divine in his beloved's embrace. He experiences his spiritual nature in his beloved's flesh and blood; each of their bodies is a wondrously valuable material thing that also refers beyond the physical plane to a transcendent All.

While Campbell restricts amor to this physical and spiritual love between two people, it is also theoretically possible to envision it in the agapetic context of loving everyone in particular. As a culture we need to retain an amorous connection to everyone, and not disconnect the erotic element from the loving experience as Christian theorists often try to do.

Amor, in this full and expansive sense, seems to be what Martin Buber, the Jewish mystic and philosopher, means when he speaks of the "I-Thou" relationship.[45] In the I-Thou relationship, as opposed to the I-it relationship, each person values the other as a full person, in the comprehensive context of his or her strengths and weaknesses. This I-Thou relationship can be extended to the whole of nature, as premodern cultures such as those of the Native Americans testify. The creatures of the natural world, even the planet "herself" or "himself" are experienced as other body-soul combinations with whom humankind is in intimate and passionate union.

Amor, in the I-Thou love relationship, celebrates Lover energy as being at once the affirmation of individual boundaries *and* the profound transcendence of all boundaries, whether psychospiritual or physical. This formulation returns us to the Garden of Delight, and to a male's phallic means of entering it. We come back to the Freudian belief that the Child, before he is socialized into the "reality principle," luxuriates in the "pleasure principle" of "polymorphous perversity" (that is, "many-formed and all-pervasive sensual/sexual delight").[46] What he enjoys is an amorous experience of *differentiation from* and *union with* the world.

The reality principle, according to the Freudians, teaches us to deflect our primal enjoyment of love into work, and to delay the gratification of our wishes for pleasure. Often, we delay this gratification indefinitely. This brings about the tragedy of retired people who have delayed their enjoyment so long that they are too sick and too exhausted by a lifetime of labor to ever enter the Garden, at least on this side of the gates of death.

Campbell exhorts us, over and over again, to "follow our bliss." This bliss is really amor. It is the joy of feeling empowered by the Lover within to live our lives in amorous union with ourselves, with our own deepest and most central values and visions, and with others. And others—"everyone [and everything] in particular"—are, finally, One.

THE LOVER'S ORIGINS

THE MATURE MASCULINE LOVER ARCHETYPE arises from the Oedipal Child, one of the immature masculine archetypes.[1] The Oedipal Child's archetypal energy comes on line when a boy begins to become aware of his gender difference from his mother; at the same time he seeks to bond more closely with her. With this budding gender awareness, sexuality first comes into focus, along with all its attendant issues. The attempt to merge with the mother, even as the boy is feeling the need to break from her, produces enormous stresses within the young masculine psyche. In the worst instances, a father is made a marginal figure in his son's life by this intensified mother-son bonding.

Mother and Son: The Owl Goddess
and the Dependent Male

It is at this point that a father needs to step in and bring his son under the influence of nurturing masculine energy. Unfortunately, this ideal situation seldom occurs. The Oedipal Child, without any man to show him how to be appropriately sensitive, related, connected, caring, loving, and spiritual, regards all of these emerging psychic qualities as feminine. He sees them through his mother's eyes, not his father's. He may develop gender identity confusion at this point, particularly if a number of factors complicate the damage already done by the "absent father." At the very least, the Oedipal Child comes to associate all that is noblest and best in human life, all that is sweetest, gentlest, most caring and sensitive, with his mother and with her feminine realm.

A boy's semiconscious desire for his mother calls forth

the Lover. In a dynamic and creative relationship with the feminine energies, the Oedipal Child archetype empowers a boy to move in a spiritual direction. The boy who is strongly influenced by the Oedipal Child can begin to feel the wondrous vitality of Lover energy. When adequately accessed later in life by the man's Ego, the Lover becomes the source of much that is beautiful, inspiring, idealistic, and visionary in a man's life. It causes him to feel proud of his newfound masculine identity, which has been established, in the best situations, in relationship both with his mother and his father. From a Jungian point of view, it is not merely a mortal mother for whom this boy yearns—he is wired to respond to the archetypal Mother. All boys and men are wired for loving, and for mystical experience.

The ideal process of a boy's moving from the "realm of the mothers" into "the realm of the fathers" often breaks down. This is because the parents' own issues interfere with what should be a natural progress from the Oedipal Child to the adequate accessing of the mature masculine archetypes. At least in the United States, as Robert Bly points out, men have no trouble bonding with their mothers. But they do have trouble separating from them. And they can neither bond with nor separate from their fathers, because their fathers are, for the most part, unavailable—in an emotional and a physical sense. Therefore, spirituality has its origin, in modern Western culture at least, in the mother-bonded Oedipal Child.

The immature, fragmentary Shadow aspects of the archetype of the Lover "possess" an adult man when that man has not been able to move beyond the Oedipal Child. We will examine the Shadow Lover in detail in Chapters 7 and 8. For now, bear in mind only that the primary reason adult men get stuck in the Shadow Lover is that they never had older men who "held them in their hearts," as Bly says, and who helped them to find nurturing, sensitivity, relatedness, and spirituality in the context of masculine identity.

Ultimately, the Lover has his developmental antecedent, as do all the immature and mature masculine archetypes, in the Divine Child.[2] The Divine Child is what Brown and other Freudians consider the polymorphously perverse infant. The Divine Child is in complete harmony with the masculine and feminine aspects of the Self, with others, and with the world. Within the Divine Child all opposites are reconciled and integrated. Within him the life and death instincts are one, and Libido courses freely. He is the source of all our pleasure, and all our play. He is the one Jesus was referring to when urging us to be born again. In order to enter the Kingdom of Heaven, Jesus tells us, we must become like this little child.

THE LOVER AS INSTINCT

Most disarming of all, to many men, are the desires and promptings generated by the Lover. Many of us don't know how to enjoy our amorous urges without feeling overwhelmed, or emasculated by them. Men typically become comfortable with their archetypal configurations one by one, and in this order: Warrior, Magician, Lover, King. Cultural clichés about rebellious youths reflect the truth that a young man first faces the developmental task of integrating his inner Warrior. A man usually doesn't begin to consolidate his Lover structures until he reaches midlife, and the King structures, if they are addressed at all, are usually not integrated until a man is well into his fifties.

The Lover is next to last in this developmental sequence because it is so difficult an energy for most men to master. The Lover's desires frequently seem perverse or blasphemous to the Ego, which consequently does everything it can to suppress them. But those apparently perverse or blasphemous desires represent an opportunity—to redress an imbalance in the Ego's characteristic methods of dealing with the world.

The Aroused Lover: Nikkie's Invitation to a Female (Arnhem Zoo, The Netherlands)

An archetype itself is not a balanced entity. It is an impersonal configuration.[3] An archetype isn't "nice." Rather it has one particular desire, and it presses an imperialistic case. The Lover is happy to take over a psyche, and use it to fulfill all of its often reckless desires. Left alone, the Lover is no more concerned for the Warrior, Magician, or King than they are for him. The Ego must step in and mediate between these structures. Otherwise we remain unconscious of them, and we allow impersonal patterns and instincts to live our lives for us.

Archetypes represent the *potentials* of the human animal. We are unique, as animals, in the extent of our ability to become conscious of our instinctual configurations. Jung believed the crucial task of individuation was in disidentifying with these configurations, and making them conscious. By making archetypal structures conscious, we can live up to our full potentials, and draw upon the energy of an archetype only as it is needed.

But where are these structures? How is it that they arise? We endorse the theory that the archetypes arise in certain more or less specific locations in the nervous system (see Appendix B). We believe that the Lover and the other mature masculine archetypes stem from a combination of brain, nervous system, and hormonal functions. Each localizes, to some degree, in divergent neocortical structures. By manifesting the dynamics associated with those structures, the Lover, like the other archetypes, manifests certain functions that are archaic and prehuman.

At the same time, all the archetypes stimulate refined, aesthetic, and spiritualizing human functions. The biological basis for the ascent of eros may be found in the neuronal pathways of the brain. Sublimation originates in the "higher" brain function of the neocortex, from whence it exercises discriminatory control and inhibition over more primitive structures and processes.[4]

Whereas the Magician in its refined form is an expression of Left Brain functioning, the Lover is primarily an expression of Right Brain functioning. Drawing upon Right Brain modes of thought and imaging, the Lover is able instantaneously to grasp whole patterns of ideas and feelings, in contrast to the Magician's methodical mode of thought. The

Lover does his thinking in images and symbols; he gathers impressions, and experiences "leaps of imagination."

The instinct human beings have to return to the Garden of Delight can be attributed to our evolutionary origins. Animal behaviors indicate that many species share our sensual and sexual appreciation of erotic experience. Eros arises, according to some convincing data, in the limbic system, in hormonal distribution, and in the reptilian brain.

It could be argued that amorous love is a factor in the lifelong pairings of certain animals.[5] But human amor requires a greatly heightened degree of conscious awareness both of self and of the other. Because we are such stupendously complex beings, achieving and maintaining amor in our human relationships is an arduous task.

There is even evidence of altruism, a kind of agapetic love, among the higher mammals.[6] The concern and care demonstrated by mammalian mothers, and sometimes fathers, for their offspring, the giving of gifts that occurs between both children and adults in mammalian societies, and the self-sacrificial acts in which certain individuals may even give their lives for the good of the group all argue for a kind of agapetic love among mammals. Probably agape arises in the old mammalian brain (the limbic system), and is further refined in the neocortex.

"Greater love hath no man than this, that he lay down his life for his friends."[7] Campbell provides us with a dramatic example of the instinctual nature of this kind of altruism. He tells of an incident on a treacherous curve on a highway in Hawaii:

> One day, two policemen were driving up the Pali road when they saw, just beyond the railing that keeps the cars from rolling over, a young man preparing to jump. The police car stopped, and the policeman on the right

jumped out to grab the man but caught him just as he jumped, and he was himself being pulled over when the second cop arrived in time and pulled the two of them back.

Do you realize what had suddenly happened to that policeman who had given himself to death with that unknown youth? Everything else in his life had dropped off—his duty to his family, his duty to his job, his duty to his own life—all of his wishes and hopes for his lifetime had just disappeared. He was about to die.

Later, a newspaper reporter asked him, "Why didn't you let go? You would have been killed." And his reported answer was, "I couldn't let go. If I had let that young man go, I couldn't have lived another day of my life." How come?

Schopenhauer's answer is that such a psychological crisis represents the breakthrough of a metaphysical realization, which is that you and that other are one, that you are two aspects of the one life, and that your apparent separateness is but an effect of the way we experience forms under the conditions of space and time. Our true reality is in our identity and unity with all life. This is a metaphysical truth which may become spontaneously realized under circumstances of crisis. For it is, according to Schopenhauer, the truth of your life.[8]

Campbell concludes by saying that, at a deep level, altruism is fueled by the intuitive awareness that "relationship *is identity*." In other words, if you act to save another, regardless of the cost, it is because at some level you appreciate that the other is a part of your own identity. Usually the appreciation is instinctual. Most people don't consciously consider this truth, unless their religious or philosophic searchings bring them to it.

The Effeminate Christ (*The Baptism of Christ*, Masolino, 1435)

MASCULINE OR FEMININE

Throughout the cultures of the world, certain emotions and modes of thinking have been assigned to the realm of the "feminine," and others to the sphere of the "masculine." Hard-headedness, rationality, aggressiveness, and similar psychological traits have been assigned, almost universally, to men, while greater capacities for sensitivity, receptivity, and relatedness have been assigned to women. Men who are sensitive and gentle are labeled feminine, while aggressive women are called masculine. Sensitive boys are called "sissies," and rough girls "tomboys."

Evidence from studies made of very young children seems

to indicate that there *are* tendencies toward behavioral differences between boys and girls.[9] These behavioral differences may be genetically transmitted.[10] Boys tend to be more adventuresome and aggressive in their penetration of their environments; girls tend to be less competitive, and to stay closer to Mommy's lap. Hormonal changes in early puberty may accelerate these divergent psychological paths, while the very different developmental tasks boys and girls face concerning their parents (especially the mother) also contribute to what become quite different masculine and feminine psychologies.[11]

But depth psychology has made it clear that no matter how divergent we become from one another, we each carry within ourselves aspects of the other.[12] Men carry within them a feminine personality complex, called the Anima. Women bear within their psyches a masculine personality complex, called the Animus. Both the Anima and the Animus are made up of a mix of archetypal material, just as the dominant gender personality is, of emotive and complexual elements, and of culture and family-specific expectations about masculinity and femininity. These personality complexes probably have a genetic and hormonal basis.

Culture socializes boys and girls in such a way as to exaggerate the inherent differences between the sexes. The aim of such socialization is, at bottom, to encourage reproduction of the species.[13] At the same time, as feminists have pointed out, such gender "enhancement" has usually worked out to the advantage of men. Men have been granted a disproportionate amount of economic and political power.

Feminists point to "patriarchy" as the mode of culture that oppresses and subjugates women. And clearly wherever and whenever women are depreciated and oppressed, men repress their feminine, and women their masculine. Patriarchy, in this sense, leads to caricatures of the sexes which are

damaging to both men and women, and which block individuals of either sex from a full realization of selfhood. But patriarchy is no more a blank check for men as a group than it
is, in reality, the "rule of the fathers." For one thing, many of
those men who do achieve "king of the hill" status deprive
other men, as well as women, of any real sense of being worth-
while and potent. For another, often the "men" at the top are
not really men at all. They are boys pretending to be men.
Their infantilism manifests in all the horrors of history we
have come, in recent years, to associate with patriarchy.

Today, twenty years after the rise of the feminist movement, after all of the reevaluation of gender roles and identities in which we have been engaged, men and women are
wondering what exactly does make them different from each
other. What, if anything, makes men masculine and women
feminine?

Many male chauvinists still make the claim that the sexes
can be divided in a simple way, in their emotional and cognitive modes, along traditional lines. But radical feminists are
often as guilty of caricature as are their male chauvinist counterparts. One can read a great deal of feminist literature and
never encounter a single statement of appreciation for traditional masculine virtues. Men as a sex are demonized and
slandered as the source of all neurosis and psychopathology.
While these feminists attack men for their power drives, aggressive behaviors, and insensitivity, they grant to women all
the noble, kind, and tender virtues. In their eyes, all men are
bad boys, and women have no Shadows. Such a point of view
is every bit as one-sided and pathological as the male chauvinist view that men are superior to women. The feminist attack,
whether strident and confrontational (as in the writings of
Mary Daly), or subtle (as in Riane Eisler's *The Chalice and
the Blade*), amounts to the same thing. Feminine traits are
good, masculine traits are bad.[14]

Such chauvinism, whether of the male or of the female

variety, still begs the question of what masculinity and femininity are. How are they different? We might be better off if we dispensed with these stereotyped terms.

In the Far East the terms *yin* and *yang* are used to describe the bipolar dynamic of aggressive and receptive urges in the human self. Modern brain research describes a very real dichotomy in the emotive and cognitive modes of the two hemispheres of the cerebral cortex. This dichotomy seems related, to some extent, to the yin and yang of the psyche. Again, from a Jungian point of view, both men and women live out their masculine and feminine energies in their bodies and their psyches. While men may experience more yang energy than yin, and women more yin than yang, it is still true that each sex draws on the energies more typical of the opposite sex for fullness of being. A man cannot be fully masculine, in a mature way, without being in an intimate and creative relationship with his Anima.

When we relate this discussion of divergent emotive and cognitive modes to the mature masculine archetype of the Lover, we need to ask whether the Lover arises out of so-called feminine psychological characteristics—relatedness, nurturing, caring, tenderness, sensitivity—or out of a masculine psychological background that includes such characteristics. Is there anything inherently feminine about the above qualities? Or are they just as much the province of masculinity as of femininity? After all, Dionysus, one of the Lover's aspects, displays feminine characteristics. Krishna, in Hindu paintings, has markedly feminine features. His soft lips, almond eyes, and soft blue body all create the impression of femininity. Yet the maenads go crazy for Dionysus and the gopis are enchanted by Krishna. Jesus, a sexless aspect of the Lover, is often depicted as a rather feminized young man. He is also surrounded by women, even though ostensibly there are no erotic wishes passing between him and them.

But the Lover has other faces. Bawdy satyrs, the "horny"

Krishna and the Gopis (Kishangarh painting, circa 1775)

centaurs, blood-red Priapus, athletic Eros, and muscle-hardened Vishnu are all his expressions. And Shiva is often imaged as a mighty, world-creating *lingam*.

In our modern iconography of the Lover we find the aggressive and feverish Elvis, who nonetheless has doe eyes, and wants to be loved "tender" and "true." There is the pretty boy, Julio Iglesias, who is reputed to have left a trail of broken hearts behind him, the result of his "savaging" of the tender emotions of his female devotees. And there is the rough and rowdy Sinatra, who charms women with his boyish smile.

To the extent that the archetypal Lover is incarnate in these and other celebrated men (who are "stars" because they glow with the radiance of an archetypal charge), he appears to be a strange and compelling mixture of masculine and feminine characteristics. *We believe that the Lover has not eschewed his masculine, or yang energy, but rather is in harmonious relationship with his yin energy. Men who are accessing the Lover are no less masculine than men who are not.* Paradoxically, to the extent that they have been able to

embrace their yin energy, their yang has actually been en-
hanced. In the Lover, *masculine* energy is tender, gentle,
related, nurturing, and caring in its own way. Masculinity, in
other words, is not the same as emotional frigidity, hard-
headed rationality, and brutality.

The men's movement today has revealed that many men,
at least in the United States, have gotten in touch with their
"softness," but that they have become profoundly unhappy in
the process. Many say that they have been taught, primarily by
feminists, that masculine power is a bad thing. According to
its detractors, masculine aggressiveness must be eliminated.
Those who seek to shame it, often women, fail to realize that
they themselves are as aggressive as their male targets. Aggressiveness, while it may be boosted by male testosterone,
is not limited to men.[15] Depressed men, if they protest against
the aggressive treatment they receive at the hands of angry
women, are often haunted with vindictive questions such as,
"What's the matter? Do you feel intimidated? Do you feel
castrated?" Shamed men do not make good lovers. They
become "nice boys." Any show of masculine assertiveness
automatically makes them "bad boys." These and other
disempowered men have fallen back into the sphere of the
Mother. They have regressed into the Oedipal conflict. And of
course they do not feel they can make love to their "mothers."

*These men have accepted the idea that masculinity, in
its essence, is hurtful and destructive, while femininity, in its
essence, is loving and generative.* And yet the men's movement is demonstrating that mature masculinity is strong, aggressive, hard-headed, and receptive, gentle, and emotive, all
at the same time. When a man is less than this it is because his
psyche has been co-opted by the immature masculine archetypes. The Lover, then, is fully masculine. He transcends the
caricatures of masculine and feminine, and ecstatically unites
yin and yang in the psyches and bodies of mortal men.

THE LOVER AND THE OTHER ARCHETYPES
OF THE MASCULINE SELF

At first glance, the Lover seems to be fundamentally opposed to the other three mature masculine archetypes. The King, the Warrior, and the Magician all stand for creative ordering and structure, though in characteristically different ways. The Lover seems to undermine structure. He champions the pleasure principle over the reality principle, play over work. Ecstasy, by its very nature, transcends boundaries and structures. Campbell frankly says that "illicit" love is love's highest form—that is, love that defies structure. Historically, lovers of truth and knowledge, whether scientists whose discoveries challenge the prevailing concepts, or artists and musicians who critique the norms of ordered society, always rub the establishment the wrong way. The first groups that any oppressive tyranny persecutes are the artists and the intellectuals.

Sam Keen, in *The Passionate Life*, describes the stages of love. Keen believes that human beings are made for love, and that different forms of love come into play at different stages in the human life cycle. One of the most important forms of love, according to Keen, is the "Outlaw."[16] This form of the Lover manifests markedly antistructural characteristics. Arising for the first time in adolescence, the Outlaw is present in the rebel idealist who strikes out against societal norms. The rebel is a young man who clings to an ideal of truth and beauty for which he would gladly give his life. His ideal could be a political cause, a religious vision, or a woman. Outlaw Lover energy recalls Hegel's antithesis—it challenges the ossifying structural thesis and forces it to yield to new possibilities. The

The Outlaw Lover:
Marlon Brando

rebel Lover keeps things active, and is open to new influxes of
Libido, fresh from the fires of creation deep in the unconscious. He opens the eyes of the Magician to the sudden,
unforeseen break in the earth-plane, through which the life-
giving power of the divine pours out onto a parched wilderness
and causes the desert to bloom. He engenders love between
individuals who would never have been caught dead together
otherwise.

In breaking the ethical boundaries by which people regu-
late their lives, the Lover opens up the possibility of loving

more deeply and authentically. The archetypal Lover, as incarnate in Jesus, challenged the ethics of first century A.D. Judaism; men and women, the pious and the irreligious, the Jews and the "heathen," had ordered their lives with a categorical civility. Jesus broke down the categorical barriers, and radicalized the Torah. He interpreted it to mean that we must love the "lost" and "the least" within ourselves and within others. The Lover today, as expressed in the modern psychoanalytic process, teaches us to value those parts of ourselves that we have thrown away in the process of becoming socialized into the structures of society. By revaluing what cultural norms have devalued, we learn compassion for ourselves and for others.

In this paradoxical sense, the Lover is amoral, but is also the source of *authentic* morality. And it is the Lover's refusal to accept the artificiality of boundaries—within the psyche and between people—that is the source of the sense of relatedness from which familial and societal structures arise *in the first place*. Freud's Superego, although apparently at odds with the Lover, turns out to be one manifestation of his energy.

The other three mature masculine archetypes need the Lover in order to avoid falling into sterility, schizoid manifestations, or sadism. The Lover provides them, through his passionate valuing of the other, with their generativity and their reason for being. Because of his regard for the other, he keeps them from remaining immature and narcissistically self-involved. He gives the King the passion to make a world, and provides him with the "creative" aspect of the creative ordering that is the hallmark of the ruler on the Primal Hill. The Warrior draws from the Lover motivation for the aggressive pursuit of good, and for wielding his sword against the King's enemies, chaos and death. And the Lover provides the Magician grounds for stewarding the sacred space the Lover reveals, and for aiding human beings in their quest for initiation into healed and more integrated ways of living.

The Lover needs the other three archetypes to keep him moral. He needs to experience the value of their structures and the vital importance of boundaries. He needs the "artificiality" of form which each of them invokes and imposes in order to channel his Libido in productive ways. The Lover uses the bounded channels established by the other three archetypes for moving from the eternal infinite into the finite temporal world. He needs the other mature masculine archetypes in order to incarnate in such a way as to enhance human life, rather than destroy it in an uncontained cascade of light and ecstasy.

5

HIS PATH THROUGH
THE GARDEN

THE MATURE MASCULINE ARCHETYPE OF THE Lover moves from an eternal into a finite world through a variety of channels. He has a place in every man's life, and we have all had experience of him. But certain occupations seem particularly likely to draw upon the Lover's energies. At the center of the Garden of Delight, the Lover is bursting with images, symbols, dreams, and visions, and an ultimate ecstasy beyond words. From the Tree of Life he plucks the fruit of generativity and tosses it over the Wall of Paradise to mortal poets, prophets, mystics, artists, and connoisseurs, who eagerly await his gifts. We turn our attention now to these men,

The Lover and His Beloved in the Garden:
Krishna and Radha in an Amorous Embrace
(Kangra painting, India, late eighteenth century)

to see how they work to embody the Lover; from their experiences we may derive a finer understanding of the archetype's characteristic modes.

THE LOVER AND THE WORD

The creative Word rings out from the Gate at the Garden Wall. The Word was first celebrated as a means of cosmogony by the ancient Egyptians,[1] and it was from them that the biblical authors derived semi-magical incantations such as: "And God *said*, let there be light, and there was light."[2] The Word is the concrescence of the illimitable. It creates form from formlessness. By *words* we see and make the world—both our inner worlds and the outer worlds around us. At the Garden's Gate the Lover meets the Magician, who tends the boundaries of the sacred space within the Wall. The Lover "gives the word" to the Magician. And there, where the energies of the Lover and the Magician interpenetrate, the mind and heart of the poet burst into visionary flames. He runs from the scene, burdened with the imperative to speak his revelation: "Thus saith the Lord!" or "Allah commands!" or "Who, if I cried out, would hear me among the angels' hierarchies?"[3]

The Magician enables limitless Libido to take concrete form in the world. Carefully crafting the verbal building blocks of consciousness, the Magician enables the "Unmanifest Brahman"[4] to become manifest. He allows the "Christ Consciousness"[5] in all of us, the Essence of Mind, to incarnate in our finite human neuronal pathways. By restraining the Lover's titanic powers, the Magician empowers a man such as William Blake to sing of the Lamb and the Tiger, almost in the same breath.[6] From the Lover, Shakespeare secures the power to spin words from thin air for weaving his spells of enchantment; Walt Whitman acquires the ability to find the shimmering in the leaves of grass "divine."[7] Kahlil Gibran gets from the Lover the power to penetrate the veil of matter, and show the sad beauty beneath the things of this world; Wallace Stevens whirls peacock feathers around the room while palm shadows dance and Susanna is ravished by the old men.[8]

The Lover, pushing hard against the boundaries the Magician establishes around him, opens a world of insight for the tarot card reader, teleports the psychic's inner eye a thousand miles and shows him impossible visions, and reveals to the prophet hidden sources of corruption and the wellsprings of healing. It is the Lover who clutches Mohammed by the throat and commands him, "Recite, recite."[9]

The Lover rises up in the middle of the night and offers the scientist in his dreaming the last piece of a mental puzzle. He moves the chalk in the mathematician's hand, drawing, through him, "rumors of angels" on the blackboard. And it is the Lover who lures the physicist toward the dawn of time and space, promising to deliver an "elegant theory" which will demonstrate, finally, the properties of the Planck Era.

The musician and the composer hear the voice of the Lover singing from another world. It seems so far away, separated by such a high and impenetrable Wall, and yet, it is "closer than breathing and nearer than hands and feet."[10] Guided by the Magician's system of musical notation, the composer translates the Lover's song into marks on a piece of paper. By following these marks instrumental artists recreate something like the original song, so that we, too, can hear the voice of the Lover.

THE LOVER IN MYSTIC EXPERIENCE

At the Garden Wall all words fail, unable to penetrate the scented air, hushed by the sounds of the quiet "Joy beyond the bonds of the world."[11] The mystics, from all religions and from all times and places, come here to challenge the gate-keepers, push aside the flaming sword that "turns this way and that"[12] to keep us out of Paradise, and hear the Lover's words. Some lose their way and never return to our world. Others stagger from the Gate, hair whitened, a faraway look in their eyes. They struggle to speak, to tell us things that are beyond mortal words. They stammer and fall silent. Still others, the writing mystics, like Nicholas of Cusa, Meister Eckhart, St. Bernard, the Sufis, and the authors of the Hindu *Upanishads*,

The Musician Embodying the Lover: Nyama Suso
Reciting with *Kora* Accompaniment

find words sufficient to at least outline the experience of the
Garden, so that others can find their way.

According to Cusa, Paradise beyond the Wall is pure
unity, and is rich simultaneously in diversity. It is the same
sacred space as the pure unity of Nirvana, the light-filled
Essence of Mind of the Buddhists, the Unmanifest Brahman
of the Hindus, the Pleroma of the Gnostics, and the collective
unconscious of the depth psychologists. It is the "peace which
passes understanding"—and understanding's verbal structures. At the same time, the Garden is filled with every single
differentiated finite being, atoms and molecules, zebras and
galaxies. As each thing "held in the heart"[13] of the Lover is
called by name, it manifests on this side of the Wall, in space
and time. For the mystic adequately accessing the Lover,
things do not lose their value because they have become mate-

The Pool—Apache: The Lover at One with Nature (Edward S. Curtis, 1868–1952)

rial. Nature is all one in time and space, and the creatures of nature are loved for what they are—rock, mineral, pulp, or flesh and blood.

The mystic loves both expressions of the Lover energy: nature as multiplicity, and as unity. Thus, the Lover is the source of both spiritual and natural mysticism. He knows the beloved as God and as the World. He loves "everyone in particular," *both* the lion and the lamb. And he loves everything as a whole. The Lover is the source of the ecological vision of a green earth. He is the Gardener of Eden.

In the biblical book of Genesis, Yahweh is the original Gardener. But the Shadow falls with the coming of consciousness to Adam and Eve. In the New Testament, the Garden is restored when Mary, in mystic vision, sees through her tears the risen Christ. She takes him—rightly—for the gardener.[14]

Chief Seattle of the Puget Sound Indians, when he was pressured by the white men to sell them a part of what is now the state of Washington, is said to have written a letter to their president.[15] Whether or not this letter is apocryphal, it expresses the Lover's understanding of humankind in the world of nature:

> How can you buy or sell the sky, the warmth of the land? If we do not own the freshness of the air and the sparkle of the water, how can you buy them? Every part of the earth is sacred to my people. Every shining pine needle, every sandy shore, every mist in the dark woods, every clearing, and humming insect is holy in the memory and experience of my people. The sap which courses through the trees carries the memories of the red man. . . . We are a part of the earth and it is a part of us. The perfumed flowers are our sisters; the deer, the horse, the great eagle, these are our brothers. The rocky crests, the juices in the meadows, the body of heat of the pony, and the man—all belong to the same family. . . . The earth is our mother. Whatever befalls the earth befalls the sons of the earth. Man did not weave the web of life, he is merely a strand in it. Whatever he does to the web, he does to himself.[16]

These are things that poets, prophets, and seers continually rediscover. The "new age" movement today is alive with Lover energy, generating a new hunger for both his spiritual and natural ways. Concern for the health of the environment is united with a renewed sense of the sanctity of the created world. At the same time, new age religions encourage their followers to delve more deeply into their inner worlds. From Greenpeace to analytical psychology, from the new cosmology to "creation spirituality," the Lover's many aspects are revealed, once again, to contain both diversity and unity, body and soul.

The Artist Embodying the Lover

THE LOVER AND THE ARTIST

The forms and colors by which the visual artist renders concrete the ineffable are preverbal. This may place the visual artist in closer proximity to the archetype of the Lover than the users of language—poets, prophets, mathematicians, composers, and philosophers. At the very least, the visual artist, like these others, has a struggle on his hands, as he labors to embody in playful yet disciplined processes the infinite in finite productions. The visual artist appropriately accessing the Lover becomes a conduit for the incarnation of wordless wonder—the terror and beauty of a superabundance of Libido—which seeks to pour into this world through form and color.

The cultural and creative achievements of the artist make us human. They make life in the world worth living. The artist personifies open-ended and continuous transformation, and offers to his fellow creatures that same transformational possibility. In psychological development, transformation of the individual is guided by archetypal structures and dynamics. The universal drive of the species toward transformation—toward both greater diversity and greater unity—expresses itself in the paths of individuals, and none more so than the individual artist.

Jung pointed out that neuroses and complexes attack and wound the Ego along its path to transformation. These partial personalities are emissaries of the Self, which will not tolerate any one-sided or exaggerated attitudes on the part of the Ego, and will not abide either psychological splitting or moralistic rigidity. What is true for the individual psyche is also true for the collective psyche as it is expressed through culture.

As Erich Neumann writes in *Art and the Creative Unconscious*, whenever a complex of the personal unconscious leads to achievement instead of neurosis (or, we would argue, *through* neurosis to achievement) the individual becomes, in the broadest sense, an artist. He becomes creative. The original feeling of inferiority or worthlessness, and the resulting compensatory "will to power" which cuts through it, are not arrested in pathological fantasies. Instead they go on to incarnate something of collective significance. The neurotic fantasies that complexes generate, while they may be as one-sided and as extreme as the attitudes and values of the Ego, are always ultimately in the service of a Self which aims at greater psychological wholeness. And if these fantasies are given form by the artist, then they open the artist's personality, and through him the collective psyche, to creative advance.

If the artist can allow himself to temper his visions with the reality principle, his fantasies result in cultural and artistic achievements. These achievements break past the repression barrier erected by the Superego. The artist who is continuously open to the liquefying effects of Libido hurls himself, through his works, against the rigidity of established structures. Cultural rigidity manifests in many forms, in artistic canons, inhuman laws, religious and political dogmatisms, closed economic systems, repressive codes of ethics, and in ecological exploitation. The artist, in his structure-challenging role, exemplifies the Outlaw Lover in action.

The Lover manifests himself to the artist ideally, not as an "irruptive possession" of his Ego, but as a generative power that relates the Ego-consciousness to the Self, what Edward Edinger calls an "Ego-Self axis,"[17] in which consciousness and the powers of the unconscious mingle freely. The Ego, stewarded by the structuring, striving, and containing archetypes of the King, the Warrior, and the Magician, accesses the libidinal energy of the Lover. This generative connection between Ego-structure and the boundary-defying Lover becomes, in Buber's terms, an I-Thou relationship in which the Ego's "I" meets in mutual celebration the Lover's (ultimately, the Self's) "Thou." Artistic productions are always the result of this inner I-Thou relationship.

Neumann believes that the world the artist images as a result of this I-Thou relationship is the world of the Child. It is the world of "the primordial one reality, not yet split by consciousness."[18] It is the Garden beyond the Wall. Great works of art "grow transparent" to this underlying "unitary reality." They reveal the "Is-ness," as Meister Eckhart called it, behind the "Becoming" of finite entities in space and time. At the same time, great works of art also revel in the process of becoming what all things already *are* on the other side of the Garden Wall.

Artists are often perceived to be childlike. Some seem even childish—for example, Salieri's view of Mozart in *Ama-*

deus typifies the impression Westerners often have of their artists. For the artist, regression to a childlike state of deep communion with the realm of the archetypes, in which everything is filled with cosmic import and power, is in the service of a *progression* toward cultural and artistic achievement. Through his creations the artist unifies the archaic level of the instincts with the spiritual level of ideals. This is a mighty achievement indeed, especially in light of the profound alienation our modern schizoid culture suffers from our instinctual roots. It is this imaging of human wholeness, of the lost paradise of childhood, that gives art its captivating power. The symbols that the artist expresses on canvas, in wood or stone, or in any other medium, reflect dimensions of meaning and realms of feeling that transcend analytic thought.

Perhaps surprisingly, psychoanalysis has tended to derive the artist's creativity from either his "excess of Libido," or his lack of adequate Ego-structures. It is true that the developmental history of the artistic child is problematic, but Jungians take a more positive view of the budding artist's developmental issues than do most Freudians. For Jungians, "in the wound is the opportunity."

As Neumann points out, the creative child remains in touch with the childhood world of archetypal realities, while other children gradually become socialized into the "real" world. Most children learn the importance of relinquishing "toyland" and accepting the "do's and don'ts" of the social world. They succumb to the pressures of the Superego and adopt the adult experience of reality—wherein a myriad of finite entities compete with each other for finite rewards. The majority of children, in other words, repress the pleasure principle and adopt the labor-intensive reality principle. They learn that trees are not magic, that there is no Santa Claus, and that such things as truth and beauty are only marginally significant. The potential artist, however, retains his sense of the magic that animates the things of this world. He knows that the world is alive, not an empty mechanism. He will not give up the primordial sense of vividness and wholeness with which he came into this world. He recognizes his personal wholeness, in which no part of his body or of his psyche is shamed and repressed, as well as the wholeness and interconnectedness of all things.

His inability or unwillingness to give up his original unitary worldview drives his parents to distraction. They and the society which supports their own fragmented personalities—in which instinct and feeling are split off from Ego and "mind"—condemn the artistic child as a dreamer. In his teenage years he becomes a bum, a hippie, a good-for-nothing. Yet he remains loyal to his original image of wholeness. He continues to believe that there is harmony behind the apparent competition. If he can work through the neuroses that the enormous pressures to split foist upon him, the artist, as a man, will be able to show to himself and to the society that has attacked him the magical power of the One in the Many.

Neumann follows the traditions of Western culture in terming the archetypal world of the collective unconscious the realm of the mothers, and the world of Ego-conscious "reality" the realm of the fathers. He believes that the mother with whom the artist is so stubbornly bonded is the archetypal Mother, and not simply his mortal mother. Neumann claims that the explanation for the artist's unusual creativity lies in his intense interaction with his own inner feminine—his Anima—a part of which he experiences as his Mother.

The problem raised by Neumann's characterization of the artist's bond with the Mother is a problem we addressed before: Is the Lover essentially feminine or masculine? On the island of Bali, people regard the origin of the artist's creativity in quite a different light. Male mask-makers and dancers, for example, ascribe their creative powers to their fathers rather than to their mothers.[19] On Bali, artistic expression is not linked to the concept of femininity any more than it is linked to presumed masculine traits.

In Freudian terms, the artist may be less repressed than other personality types. In Jungian terms, the artist may be living out a more fully developed Ego-Self axis than are the majority of his peers. In any case, whether the other within is thought of as Mother, as Father, as the personal and the collective unconscious, as the Divine Child, the Anima, or the Self—or as aspects of all of the above—the artist is drawn by the terrifying and enchanting power of the Lover into an incarnational process. Through suffering, self-sacrifice, and transports of ecstasy, this process leads a fragmented psyche back to the Garden, and empowers others who have "eyes to see and ears to hear"[20] to follow in the quest for wholeness.

CONTEMPORARY ART AS EMBODIMENT
OF THE LOVER

Many of the works of premodern art clearly reveal the life-force of the Lover. The gaily colored tomb paintings of ancient Egypt are electric and lively. The sensuous, undulating phallic art of the Mayas, the frankly erotic stonework of the great Hindu temple at Konarak, the seductively smiling colossi of Angkor Wat—these and many other works of ancient artists reveal the presence of the Lover in all his amorous creative power. Botticelli's *The Birth of Venus* astounds us by the sheer force of its Lover-inspired beauty, a powerful combination of sensuously archaic and spiritualized, idealistic aspects of eros. Even Rembrandt's somber studies in light and shadow display a passionate, if dark, love for the human soul. The joyful exuberance of the Impressionists, the nostalgic enchantment of Maxfield Parrish's storybook illustrations, the captivating nudes of Gauguin—we feel the Lover, like the grace of God, in all of these. But can we see contemporary art as an expression of the Lover?

Aniela Jaffé, one of Jung's early disciples, brilliantly and comprehensively analyzes the works of modern artists from a depth psychologist's perspective in her essay "Symbolism in the Visual Arts."[21] We will be guided by her remarks in our brief discussion of the Lover and the modern artist.

Modern art is often characterized as imaginative, as abstract, or as nonfigurative. Modern artists do not tend to reproduce objects in the natural world in a realistic way. When they do, they do so in unconventional ways. Art that uses "found objects," for instance, places those objects in unnatural surroundings. The surrealists use recognizable representations of objects, but bend and twist them to make symbolic statements.

The artist is a spokesperson for his age. Modern artists of significance plumb the depths of the collective unconscious in order to give expression to an inner vision of the human soul and to "the spiritual background of life and the world."[22] This is why the forms and colors they use often do not realistically reflect the things of this world. The modern artist is striving to picture for us a hidden reality *behind* the reality we take for granted. The outer colors and forms are means to an inner, transformational end.

Paul Klee said that an object in art "awakens our love just because it seems to be the bearer of powers that are greater than itself."[23] Modern artists, like the mystics, seem to believe in a "spirit in matter" which matter partly reveals and partly obscures. Giorgio de Chirico, the founder of the *pittura metafisica* school of Italian art, wrote that "every object has two aspects: The common aspect, which is the one we generally see and which is seen by everyone, and the ghostly and metaphysical aspect, which only rare individuals see at moments of clairvoyance and metaphysical meditation. A work of art must relate something that does not appear in its visible form."[24] Franz Marc wrote in a similar vein that the goal of art now must be "to reveal unearthly life dwelling behind everything, to break the mirror of life so that we may look being in the face."[25]

Such statements by modernists manifest a profoundly spiritual motive in their work. But clearly they also reveal a danger. While St. Paul may long for that time when he can turn from the mirror in which he sees "darkly," and behold the divine "face to face,"[26] religious traditions and depth psychology alike warn of the danger to the Ego of coming fully into the divine presence. Ego-structures can be annihilated by the sheer unrestrained force of archetypal energies. Semele was instantly consumed by fire when she beheld the face of Zeus,[27] and the ancient Hebrews knew that no man could see the face of God and live.[28]

The danger of getting too close to the dark fire of the unconscious is graphically portrayed by many works of modern art, from de Chirico's faceless (and therefore unconscious) representations of the human figure to Dali's *The Burning Giraffe*. Giacometti's elongated stick figures seem to have been charred in a nuclear fire, and Jackson Pollock's chaotic paintings are as unsettling as a madman's ravings. Many works of modern art seem to loom above us in our galleries, haunting us with our own unspoken and nightmarish fears.

There is little doubt that the artists who create these images are giving form to the dark anxieties of our modern world. They are showing us just how alienated we are from our instinctual roots and how dangerous to our continued survival the products of our "scientific" unconsciousness are. We catch a glimpse in their work of a vengeful collective unconscious compensating for the arrogance of the "rational"

Ego. Repressed, the Lover becomes dark, orgiastic, and annihilating. When we try to bind him, Dionysus hurls us back into the infinite sea of the unconscious, from which there may be no return. With his insistence on the interconnection of all things, with his demand that we recognize the *value* of all things, the Lover will consent to be guided by reasonable structures. But he will not accept being split off and repressed.

Modern artists receive projections of disowned Lover energy from the rest of society. This may put the artist in a vulnerable and masochistic position, which he may not be aware he is maintaining. People often maintain friendships with artists in order to avoid the responsibility of carrying and channeling creative and prophetic energy themselves.

Depth psychology has demonstrated that what is repressed will return, and that it will rarely return in a pleasant form. A dark and cthonic eros, split off and repressed by a society of workaholics, has returned to our broken world with a vengeance. The stockpiles of nuclear weapons and the effects of massive pollution are testimony to the rage of denied eros, as surely as the products of the many modern artists who seem to be possessed by the Lover's dark side.

Marc Chagall descended into his own inner darkness, and explored there the nightmares of the repressed Lover. Still he expresses warmth and hope in his paintings, and shows us over and over again the image of man and woman embracing in the Garden. He wrote, "Everything may change in our demoralized world except the heart, man's love, and his striving to know the divine."

Jackson Pollock, who was killed in a car accident at the age of forty-four, said that he painted in a kind of trance, completely unaware of what he was doing. His paintings, though charged with colors like "a glowing lava stream,"[29] illustrate a despair of consciousness and a nearly total possession by the incalculable power of unconscious Libido. Jaffé writes that Pollock's paintings "seem to live in a time before the emergence of consciousness and being, or to be fantastic landscapes of a time after the extinction of consciousness and being."[30] However brilliant they may be, Pollock's paintings bode the same ill for the collective psyche as they did for his personal life.

Strangely and wonderfully, just at the point at which consciousness and structure seem to disappear into the darkness of the body and the death instinct, light appears and the Lover's life instinct reasserts itself. Uncannily, Pollock's canvases resemble nothing so much as the microphotographic images of the once hidden structures of organic and inorganic matter. At the bottom of the well of chaos there lies a realm of primordial organization. A safety net appears beneath our feet. The Lover reveals himself once again in a joyous riot of form and color in the microscopic world underlying the larger world in which we live. Purposefulness and orderliness lie hidden in the deep realm from which body and soul arise from each other and follow their differing paths.

THE LOVER AND APPRECIATIVE CONSCIOUSNESS

Most of us are probably not artists in the narrow sense of the term, nor are we mystics. But we are all participants in "appreciative consciousness." We are all, in some area and to some extent, connoisseurs. To the extent that we can genuinely appreciate the beauty and pleasure of anything, we are in touch with the Lover, following one of the paths in his Garden.

There are many paths to the Self at the center of the primordially whole psyche. Hindus are encouraged early in life to choose a particular God out of the vast pantheon of Gods and Goddesses available to them. Once he has chosen a "patron saint," a Hindu will follow that one Deity, and the life-style he or she prescribes, to the end of his life. There the one God who is the goal of all the Gods and Goddesses and of all created things stands revealed. Hindus are sensuously involved with their Gods. Flowers, ornaments, incense, oils, and brightly colored offerings are all part of the Hindu approach to divinity. While "God" (the Self) transcends the world of the senses, the Deity also delights in the "dance of Maya" (the material world). As Hinduism teaches, we are all Brahman playing at being ourselves.[31] Our task is to follow the clues he has left us in the world of the senses in order to "remember" who and what we really are. Thus, whatever path we follow, we will all ultimately arrive at the same sacred space.

In the depths of the psyche, according to Jungians, all the archetypes, immature and mature, masculine and feminine, embrace in amorous harmony. It is a harmony that is vivid, dynamic, calm, and joyful. As the archetype of sensuality, the Lover encourages human beings to take the paths of physical and psychological pleasure. He encourages us to delight in the things of this world, and to enjoy our Libido: eros, agape, and amor.

He inspires the connoisseur who relishes the things that stimulate the senses. The Lover urges us to taste, touch, smell, hear, and behold the beautiful, the pungent, the mellifluous, and the serene. Fine wines, vintage cars, Cuban cigars, exotic foods, silk shirts, even feeling-toned ideas—the Lover inspires our cherishing of these wonders of the sensual world. He spurs on collectors, those men who find pleasure in gathering stamps, coins, memorabilia, antiquities, baseball cards, finely crafted weapons, books, even pornographic magazines—these and many other objects and images serve as icons of the Self, as colorful and fragmentary reminders of a once and future wholeness.

"Buffs" and "enthusiasts" draw their sense of fascination for the objects and activities of their enthusiasms from the

Lover. Favorite sports and pastimes, hobbies, research into historical epochs—all these activities reveal the Lover within. "Fans"—of certain kinds of music and musical groups, of political candidates, of particular ethnic and cultural traditions, of TV series—are all following different paths the Lover has laid into the Garden of Delight.

If connoisseurs, collectors, enthusiasts, and fans could become aware of the unconscious intent of their fascinations, they would be able to draw closer to the source of these enthusiasms. They could more intentionally embrace the Lover within. In this way, they could initiate a conscious program whose aim would be to make them more whole. Like the Hindus who select one God and follow him or her to the "font of life," these men could discover that paradise is located *within their own bodies, minds, and souls.*

THE LOVER IN RELATIONSHIP

In the magic of fully engaged lovemaking a man and his partner simultaneously affirm their separate identities and lose their individuality to a wider, deeper, and higher dimension. The act carries them, however briefly, into the mystery of the origins of all things. Procreation is among the aims of lovemaking, though it is certainly not the only aim. But it seems as if we have to touch the mysterious substrate from which all things arise and into which, as Jaffé says, "consciousness and being" subside, in order to evoke a new finite entity—the child that can issue from our union.

For the King, lovemaking aims primarily at procreation. Its purpose is to provide an heir and ensure the fertility of the kingdom. Lovemaking for the Warrior manifests as erotic conquest and as release from the tensions of combat. The ascetic Magician's lovemaking is nearly totally inner-directed,

Ecstatic
Embrace

though he may know agape love for others.[32] The Lover, as he filters through these other archetypal configurations, inspires them all. But lovemaking for the Lover himself, while it can involve spiritualized eros and agape, always also involves an amorous physical union between human beings.

The most integrated form of love comes from the mature and fully expressed Lover. A man adequately and appropriately accessing the Lover within cannot experience his lovemaking in fragmentary form. He cannot limit it to a meeting of minds (as in Platonic love), nor to a meeting of hearts (as in agapetic love). Nor can he restrict his lovemaking to a simple meeting of bodies. His lovemaking encompasses all forms of love. He will not be blocked in his amorous behaviors by a "mother complex," nor will he sublimate his eros in response, perhaps, to a castrating woman. Rather, he will know and live the passion of the ancient Canaanite God Ba'al for his bride Anath.[33] He will understand the Hindu *Kama Sutra* with the wisdom of instinct. He will feel the radiance and the pangs of amor, just as the ancient Hebrew author of the Song of Songs knew them.

THE LOVER AND PROMISCUITY

The Lover, left to his own devices, may inspire a man to be monogamous, serially monogamous, polygamous, or promiscuous. What determines the mode of a man's loving involves the ways in which he was wounded and affirmed as a boy, his resulting quest for a sense of wholeness in his masculine identity, and the degree to which he is possessed by the other major archetypes. From the standpoint of the Lover, no one mode is morally superior to another.

Monogamy remains the ideal in Western civilization, reflecting our societal interest in stable I-Thou, amorous relationships. But it is often observed that many monogamous relationships are neither meaningful nor fulfilling. People may remain married and faithful to one another, but this by no means indicates that they are accessing the Lover adequately. While it is true that the Lover can incarnate in lifelong exclusive marriages, he does so, in almost every case, quite incompletely. Furthermore, he can incarnate as well in serially monogamous, or multiple-partner settings. *We need to keep in mind that the Lover's aim is amoral in a culturally bound ethical sense. His aim is pleasure, and ultimately, ecstatic union with the All.*

It is important not to dismiss serial monogamy as merely

I and Thou (sculpture from the Hindu temple
at Konarak, India, thirteenth century)

an indication of a superficial and wandering psyche. Serial
monogamy, like monogamy, polygamy and promiscuity, can
indeed be a dead-end process. But it can equally reflect a
process of personal transformation in a man's psyche, especially concerning his experiences with others. A process of
personal transformation often involves the consolidation both
of a man's masculine identity and of his Anima. Because all
unconscious psychic material is projected onto people in the
"outer" world, a man's unconsolidated, many-faceted Anima
may appear irresistibly in a number of women, one at a time,
or in several at once. If the very foundation of the Lover's
amorality is to drive the psyche toward a complex unity, then

a series of intimate relationships, or several at the same time, may serve the Lover well. However, if a man's masculine identity is consolidated and is in intimate, safe, and creative relationship with his Anima, the likelihood *may* increase that he will prefer to maintain an exclusive, monogamous relationship with one woman, at least for an extended period of time.

Such a relationship will cost him dearly if it is dictated by societal norms, and is not an authentic expression of a man's actual psychological condition. It will exaggerate the divisions that already exist within his psyche, and it will rigidify the repression barrier that attempts either to banish the Lover or to bind him in overly narrow constraints. Such a man can easily become possessed by the bipolar Shadow of the Lover.

Yet it remains true that a man may experience psychological growth in the context of a monogamous relationship. Harville Hendrix writes, in *Getting the Love You Want*, that not only is this possible, but very likely it is the reason we fall in love in the first place. Hendrix believes that we fall in love with those who are, or seem to be, nearly identical matches for the Imago (especially in its negative characteristics) that the inner Child carries.

According to Hendrix, the task of monogamous marriage becomes getting the partner to grow in exactly the ways in which we wished our parents had grown in order to give us the love we wanted as children. We in turn must grow in order to give our partner the love she or he wanted in her or his childhood. If the Imago is matched closely enough on both sides, we each will be asked to grow in those very areas in which we were most damaged. We will heal ourselves, as well as our partner, in the process. Monogamous relationship is for Hendrix the primary setting by which the Lover can heal us and make us whole.

Once a man works through a neurosis or a complex that a particular relationship has helped to constellate, the relationship may come to lose its hold on him. If a process of mutual healing has not taken place in the relationship, the man may find his "transference issues" with respect to his partner resolved, but discover that she or he has been unable to keep up with the pace of his own transformation. Or he may find that she or he has grown too, in a way that dictates their parting. He may establish a pattern of serial monogamy as a result. The Lover within moves him out of this relationship. He may then move on into another monogamous relationship, and so on, until his various issues are resolved well enough for the consolidations mentioned above to occur.

Polygamy is officially allowed in most of the world's cultures probably for reasons that have to do with the unconscious recognition of differing male and female "reproductive strategies."[34] While underlying biological forces are almost certainly at work in polygamous and other multiple female/ single male systems, both official and otherwise, it is possible that to some extent at least these arrangements also reflect the very real difficulty most men have in realizing an integrated experience of their Animas. Often, when a man is acting out promiscuously, or having affairs, it reflects an unconsolidated Anima and, in extreme cases, chaos in the masculine Self.

Unconscious inflation and hidden grandiosity may play a role in any of the modes of loving. It is too simplistic to say that monogamy, for instance, is inherently a less inflated behavioral pattern than is promiscuity. A man may be possessed by a sense of his omnipotence, moral or otherwise, in a monogamous relationship that chronically violates his authentic experience of a cohesive Self, but that he believes he can maintain no matter what the cost to his own psychic integrity. Equally, he may be carried away by an inaccurate evaluation of his potency, or the lack of it, and act out his underlying anxiety in serially monogamous or in promiscuous behavior.

In our society, one person within a couple will usually be

unconsciously assigned the Lover energy for the couple. Both parties ought to share this responsibility for stewarding the Garden. But usually one party or another carries the burden (just as artistic friends carry other aspects of the energy). One of the first things that happens in a good course of marital therapy is that both partners begin consciously to reclaim their rejected and projected Lovers.

Midlife crises occur when one partner or another reclaims the Lover energy *unconsciously*, often outside the context of the primary relationship. This can be constructive for the individual, if he or she becomes conscious of what is happening, although it may be harmful to the relationship. The unconscious return of repressed Lover energy is more likely to be destructive the more deeply repressed it has been in the past. The energy comes back with a vengeance, often in forms almost unrecognizable as Lover energy. Eating disorders and addictions, for example, almost always signal the presence of Lover energy that has not been integrated into the personality. But before we turn to these Shadow aspects, let us examine what the Lover looks like when fully expressed.

6

THE LOVER
IN HIS FULLNESS

THE LOVER IS THE ARCHETYPE OF VIVID, SPON-taneous, and channeled Libido. Given form by the other mature masculine archetypes, the Lover makes the superabundant energy of Libido available to a man's psyche. Like the engorged phallus that is his symbol, the Lover allows the life-force to drive the psyche upward into the light of day. The Lover luxuriates eternally in the fantastic domain of the collective unconscious, behind the portals of "toyland" where the playful Child is at one with all things. Through the energies of the Lover, the conscious mind encounters the personal and collective unconscious.

For the Lover, Life Is a Carnival

(Carnival lovers in Rio)

The Lover is the archetype of *feeling*. He feels the pain and poignancy of a man's personal life, and of all living things. But no matter what his suffering, the Lover knows the fierce and terrible joy at the heart of all things.

Through his feelings, the Lover is the archetype of relatedness and of hidden connections. He knows that every fragment of the universe contains an image of the whole. Because he knows this, he is the archetype that reconciles all opposites—sensuality and intellect, pleasure and reason, body and soul, life and death, eros and agape, the Many and the One. To the extent that the King and the Magician also reconcile opposites they are drawing upon Lover energy within their own dynamic structures.

Because he sees, feels, tastes, hears, and touches the myriads of sensory forms and feeling-toned ideas, the Lover can never be convinced by limited perspectives, partial truths, or experiences that are not comprehensive. From his experience of the many he apprehends the One. Within the psyche, the Lover inspires a man to give every element, complex, and subpersonality its due, on his way toward blending them into a harmonious and unified Self. The Lover's drive is toward the unlimited, the unconditional, the uncalculating, the borderless; he moves us toward an "oceanic consciousness."

The Lover is the archetype of *desire* for pleasures that always remain unsatisfied in time and space. The essence of human being is not, as Descartes argued, in our thoughts. Rather our essence is in our desires. Desiring arises in Lover energy, and nothing can destroy it; not the reality principle, nor work, nor repression. For the Lover will always reassert himself in dreams, fantasies, and unconscious behaviors. He will always affirm the pleasure principle against whatever odds, against whatever misery of body or soul. People are not satisfied when their conscious desires are met, because they are unconscious of their real desires. The restlessness we see all around us is the restlessness of people who can smell the Garden of Delight but who do not know where to look to find it.

THE LOVER AS INSTINCTUAL DRIVE

As the *archetype of eros*, the Lover embodies in a man the hunger for sex, for sensual experience, for procreation, and for a comprehensive sense of well-being. As part of his instinctual drive the Lover "binds the soul to the sensual world," and

The Spiritualizing Lover:
At One with the Cosmos

makes of the body an "instrument of pleasure rather than work."[1]

The Lover causes a man to experience the feelings of the Divine Child in all their primordial intensity. He connects a man to the full range of his own feelings, and leaves him excruciatingly bound, in bonds of empathy and compassion, to all things. The Lover wants to touch and be touched, to hear and be heard, to smell and be smelled, to taste and be tasted, to behold and to be beheld by all.

An interesting episode in the *Star Trek* television series addresses this theme. In this episode, disincarnate aliens commandeer the bodies of a number of the *Enterprise* crew members. Once inside these sensual bodies, the aliens are overcome by a sudden uprush of desires and feelings with which they are unprepared to cope. As overpowering as these feelings are, the aliens enjoy their newfound incarnations, and do not wish to return to their disembodied condition. When they are finally forced to disincarnate and return the bodies to their rightful owners, the aliens do so with the utmost regret.

The Lover feels *the incarnation of the spirit in the things of this world*. He allows a man to experience "God" as an exotic and sensual being, present in the here and now. This awareness, which philosophers have labeled "pantheism," characterizes the religious experience of many premodern peoples. Primitive people to this day see a material world alive with the spirits of Gods, ancestors, demons, powerful shamans, and lost parts of their own psyches. The anthropologist Levi Brühl has called this sense of belonging to the underlying and animating *mana* of all finite things—trees, birds, the waving grass, the ever-changing sky—"participation mystique."[2] Psychotherapy, along with other modern sciences, regards such feelings as superstitious. We believe, however, that such feelings represent true intuitions which the Lover conveys to men who are open to the "dreaming innocence" of the inner Child.

According to Herbert Marcuse, the instinctual Lover *stands against culture and civilization*. For Marcuse, since the instincts "strive for a gratification which culture cannot grant," they are "sublimated," and their gratification indefinitely delayed.[3] Instinctually, however, the Lover wants *immediate satisfaction in pleasure, in play, in "receptiveness," and in the "absence of repression."*[4] The Lover has no interest in the reality principle, which preaches "delayed satisfaction," the "restraint of pleasure,"[5] and the engagement in work, production, and security. No matter how great our efforts to bind and banish the Lover, he remains absolutely "committed to the pleasure principle."[6]

Often men will live the first half of their lives in conformity with the reality principle, only to discover somewhere in their thirties, forties, or fifties that the repressed Lover has returned with a vengeance. They may begin acting out sexually, having affairs with their secretaries or coworkers. They may be seized by chaotic, raging, or giddy emotions, and begin to behave in ways that seem utterly foreign to them and to the people who know them. They may quit their jobs of many years and set sail for "warmer climes." They may enter a psychotherapeutic process.

If they do begin psychotherapy, they enter, in part, the sacred space of the Lover. In this sacred space, the lost Garden reappears as these men regress into childlike states of thinking and feeling. In such a process, Marcuse reminds us, "regression assumes a progressive function,"[7] since the once repressed Lover provides these startled and disoriented men with a vision of future wholeness. The "tabooed images of freedom"[8] reassert themselves and a man finds himself once more at his beginning, with his mind and heart filled with passions he thought he had long ago left behind.

The instinctual Lover drives us toward sensual and sexual *union with feminine energies and beings*. These include the inner feminine, who often makes her appearance in our erotic dreams. In these dreams our masculine Egos engage their lost feminine counterparts. The Lover does not stop here, of course, but draws us on to meet and to mate with flesh-and-blood women in the "outer" world. The sexual hunger the Lover initiates in us is one of the most basic hungers of our species. Unlike most of the other animals, human beings do not have "seasons" of sexual arousal. Barring inner or outer inhibiting factors, men and women are always ready to mate. The Lover, through the sex drive, prods us toward an eternity of pleasure.

The Mysterious Anima: Goddess of Fertility, Bread, and the
Crescent Moon

Through the Nirvana principle the Lover expresses *"the
convergence of pleasure and of death."*[9] It is the Ego that
dies, temporarily. But, for Marcuse, just as soon as eros and
thanatos converge, they diverge. He sees eros and thanatos in
the human psyche as manifesting the underlying universal
fusion and fission process which drives life. In the Nirvana
principle, says Marcuse, "the death instinct is destructiveness
not for its own sake, but for the relief of tension."[10] The flight
toward death is a flight from "pain and want." We believe it
is also a flight toward fullness of being, toward Marcuse's sense
of "integral satisfaction of needs."[11]

On the border between the Lover's drive toward archaic sensual and sexual satisfaction, on the one hand, and psycho-spiritual satisfaction on the other, the memory of the womb and the promise of "the Kingdom of Heaven" energize a man's psyche with these divergent and convergent aspects of Libido.

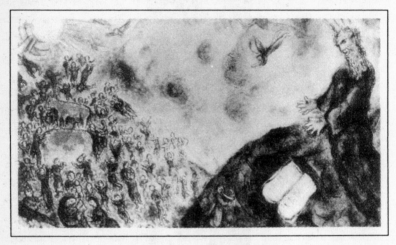

The Lover as Visionary:
Moses (Marc Chagall, 1887–1985)

THE LOVER AS PSYCHOSPIRITUAL DRIVE

Among the root hungers of the human psyche is the hunger for a sense of meaning. Spiritual experience, religious symbols, and rituals mediate this sense of meaning to the human animal. As some have theorized, humankind may be best described not as *Homo sapiens*, the "wise man," but as *Homo religiosus*, the "religious man." Without a sense that life is meaningful beyond the day-to-day struggle to survive and to propagate, most human beings, most of the time, cannot go on. They become depressed. They cannot see why they should keep pushing ahead in a world that wounds so, and so represses innate joy, and so delays the gratification of instinctual wishes.

The Lover provides the psyche with *the satisfaction of its hunger for meaning via spiritualized eros and agape.* Experiencing Nirvana, the love of God, or the Kingdom of Heaven as the Garden of Delight inspires us to love ourselves and "everyone in particular" with a truly transforming love. The Lover's passion for the intangible and the tangible, for the immortal and the mortal, draws the soul "upward."

Although the objects of his spiritual yearning and his "higher" love are spirits, souls, and ideas, the Lover provides a man's psyche with sensitivity, empathy, and a sense of connectedness to these intangibles. While the Lover energy impels us to seek and find reunion with the divine, he does so by rendering our experience of the divine and of abstract ideas sensuous. The spiritualizing Lover, so powerfully on-line in the mystics, allows us to feel the "cosmic power of harmony and life" through the things of this world, and imagine further the things of original creation.

The insights that the spiritualizing Lover imparts to a man move him to formulate metaphysical words, and to hammer these often clumsy words into relationships that will convey something of that world of unutterable delight which he has experienced. Drawing upon the idea-shaping power of the Magician, upon the impulse toward disciplined action of the Warrior, and upon the world-making skills of the King, the mystic formulates a romantic doctrine of salvation. His doctrine of salvation—of ultimate well-being—is one that heralds the *apokatastasis panton,* the "restoration of all things"[12] to the life of the Creator. Within this restoration the reconciliation of all opposites, and the resurrection of the flesh, fully incarnated by Spirit, are both accomplished. This resurrection of "Love's Body"[13] will always hold the animal and the angel, the material and the psychic, in creative and ultimately harmonious tension. Eros will be "rescued" by agape, and agape by eros. And amor will flourish as a result.

THE LOVER'S DRIVE TOWARD INCARNATION

The doctrine of incarnation, hand-in-hand with the doctrine of resurrection, is an intuitional statement of the reality of amor. In amor, spirit and body love each other fully and passionately. By urging us toward incarnating the Lover's Garden in this world, the Lover is aiming at resurrecting our primal sense of the unity of body and spirit, and our original polymorphous sense of pleasure.

Drawing upon the structuring energies of the other mature masculine archetypes to help him define, affirm, and refine his own expansive boundaries, *the Lover moves to incarnate his ecstasy in finite and bounded forms*. He moves, in the fullness of his being, to manifest himself in this world, on this side of the Wall. *Cultural achievement* is one of his manifestations—a cultural production is always an incarnational act. Something intangible is made at least partially tangible. Something potential becomes actual, something dreamed is pulled into reality.

The Lover's drive toward incarnation provides the *ethical impulse to engender harmonious order* within the individual psyche and within the institutions of society. The Lover infuses his sense of connection into the culturally developed institutions of marriage, family, friendship, and society. Reconciling the opposites of "dream" and "reality," he empowers the King to order a generative world fit for human beings to live in.

The Lover in the King, the Warrior, and the Magician is

The Lover as Radical Incarnation: *The Annunciation* (Ludovico
Carracci, 1585)

the impulse behind all forms of masculine generativity. He
offers insight and inspiration to men in all walks of life who are
striving to create new possibilities. He opens the minds of
scientists, social theorists, economists, lawyers, judges, busi-
nessmen, construction workers, politicians, and revolutionar-
ies to new opportunities. Every time a man moves to embody
in his family, profession, nation, or globe greater truth or
beauty, the Lover is seeking to plant his Garden in the here
and now. Every time any one of us acts on a hunch, or heeds
the "rumors of angels" within, we are following the lead of the
Lover.

   If the Lover, in creative union with the other mature
masculine archetypes, inspires all forms of cultural achieve-

ment, he abides, as we have seen, in an especially close relationship to the artist, writer, poet, and musician. All of these creators seek, through a process of self-sacrifice and self-transcendence, to incarnate the infinite in finite form, color, and sound. The artist holds up to us images of the Garden and so urges us to incarnate the true and the beautiful in our own worlds. The Lover, in his incarnational drive, *helps us all to be romantic about our lives*. He helps us to achieve realistic happiness, to dream possible dreams and to make them come true.

THE LOVER'S RELATIONSHIP TO LIBIDO

All of the archetypes, including the Lover, are structures of the deep unconscious. The Self is the central archetype. Each archetype gives its unique form to the underlying Libido which powers it. Libido, when poured into the form of the archetype in its fullness, and then through it into the psyche and into the created world, manifests what the Freudians call the life instinct. But when the archetype manifests in the psyche in fragmented form, it splits into a bipolar Shadow.

To the extent that psychological splitting can be seen as a "necessary" part of the Libido's simultaneous movement toward divergence (thesis, antithesis) and toward complex convergence and unity (synthesis), the bipolar Shadow forms of any archetype can be seen as opportunities for creative advance. As Jung saw, our neuroses are emissaries of a primordial and ontological Self, striving, no matter the cost, toward self-integration.

While we believe that there are four distinct forms of Libido, it can be argued that the Lover is more central to the dynamics of Libido than are the other archetypes. Freudians, in examining their archetypal configurations, might regard the

The Divine Within the Material:
The Epiphany of Hathor Among the Papyrus
(ancient Egyptian painting in the British Museum)

King, the Warrior, and the Magician as "sublimations" of Lover energy. If thinking and reflection (the Magician), delayed gratification and work (the Warrior), and the engendering of civilization and creative order (the King) are all deflections of primordial Libido, and if the Lover stands for the pleasure principle and for play, then indeed the Lover dwells closer to the fires of archaic life-force than do the other mature masculine archetypes.

At the same time, the Lover in his fullness, as expressed in the lives of mature men, draws upon the other three archetypes for his incarnational program. Therefore, the Lover him-self is sublimated to some extent. In fact, if such a thing as unconditioned Libido exists at all, it *must* be mediated and structured before passing to the psyche. It must be sub-limated, at least in part, in order for there to be a coherent psyche, and consequently a coherent created world, at all. Creation, not just civilization, demands both structure and the regulation of primordial aims, even at the level of inorganic matter. Any unmediated encounter with "pure Being" would mean the instantaneous annihilation of both consciousness and finite selves.

The archetypes, when represented as Gods, have often been depicted in sacred literature as possessing this annihilat-ing power. Any system of Ego-structure that comes into direct contact with the King, Warrior, or Magician Gods (Zeus, Yah-weh, the Gnostic "Father in the Abyss of Silence," Vishnu, and others), experiences instant fragmentation. Since these ar-chetypes primarily manifest mediating and organizing power, we believe the real source of their annihilating force lies in archetypal Libido. If the Lover is the closest of the archetypes to primordial Libido, then it is the Lover's superabundance of life-force within the King, the Warrior, and the Magician which sweeps Ego-consciousness and the created world away.

The fierce wrath of the Warrior's and the King's Shad-ows, and the cold rage of the Shadow Magician, are expres-sions of the Lover's repressed passion and frustrated Libido. This view accords well with the Freudian notion that eros and thanatos arise from the same source in Libido. It would also explain the close relationship between passion and rage in the psychological splitting present in all bipolar Shadow dis-orders, at one pole of which the Ego feels captivated by passiv-ity and ennui, and at the other pole of which—the active pole—the Ego feels possessed by feelings of aggressiveness.

CONTEMPORARY MEN AND THE LOVER

What does a man who is appropriately accessing the Lover look like? He is a man in touch with his archaic roots, with the world of childhood, with the realm of instinct, and with the promptings of his own body. He revels in his own sensuality. Simple things give him pleasure—sunlight reflected in broken glass on the street, linguine in white sauce, a tango on the radio, the smell of his lover's skin, the feel of rough wood.

He savors his feelings and does not repress them. Yet, he contains them, and maintains some cognitive distance from them, not allowing them to possess him or to plunge him into chaos. But he does *feel* them. His emotional life is not a dull gray. He is not depressed. When it is time to grieve, he does not defend against his heartbreak, pretending that everything is fine. He grieves, and is comforted knowing that his grief will pass. He endures it, and waits for release. When release comes, with a child's smile, a lover's touch, a raise at work, even with something as simple as the smell of fresh paint, he revels in it.

This man has the abiding sense that the world of things is alive. He cherishes his inner Child's feeling that spirits live in the trees, call out in the wind, look up at him from the streams, and brood on the mountaintops. He "knows" that witches ride the broomstick in the closet, and that sleighbells tinkling in the breeze signal the presence of Father Christmas.

The man appropriately accessing the Lover is in intimate relationship with all of the structures in his inner world. He honors the Child within, and will not long submit to a work situation that does not encourage the Child's play in some significant way. He accepts his Shadow aspects, without necessarily agreeing with their points of view or acting on their impulses. He loves them and compassionately views them as prodigal brothers—the lost, despised, and wounded aspects of his own true Self. Within the man accessing the Lover, Osiris and Set, Christ and Satan, and all other opposites meet, embrace, and reconcile. This man knows that life is messy, and that the good and evil urges he carries within him cannot be scrupulously divided.

He maintains a permeable repression barrier between his conscious identity and the contents of his "polymorphously perverse" unconscious. As part of this program, he is in intimate relationship with his Anima. He knows and loves her in all of her many aspects. He meets her in sexual ecstasy in his dreams, and with paper and pen he conducts regular dialogues with her. He knows that she will always be with him, and he pledges his eternal loyalty to her. The man appropriately accessing the Lover embodies what Browning calls masculine "motherliness." He becomes what Robert Bly calls a "male mother."

Through his relationships with his Child, his Shadow, and his Anima, this man offers his loving fidelity, freely and unconditionally, to the Self at the center of his psyche. He pledges his fealty to the Self, and offers his life in service to its generative purposes. This is a man who has a developed spirituality, and who embraces a vision of unity rather than one of hatred, self-righteousness, and division. While he celebrates the particular cultural, ethnic, and religious heritage into which he was born, he enjoys the diversity of human experience. He remains faithful to the Child's primordial vision that beneath diversity is an underlying unity. Spiritually, this man is a universalist, and is the true guardian of his own religion's most profound and humanizing beliefs and values.

The man appropriately accessing the inner Lover lives, as far as it is realistic for him to do so, out of his ideals, his noblest thoughts and feelings, and his dreams—for his own life, and for the life of his family, his profession, his community, his nation, and his planet.

The Lover as the Agent of Social Change: Martin Luther King, Jr.

Because he can love and care for himself deeply and authentically, he can also reach out to others with care, concern, empathy, and love. To the extent that this man has come to see all of the destructive forces human beings are up against in this life, and to the extent that he owns his own inner darkness, his love for others is real. He does not exempt himself from the human situation, or distance himself from his fellow creatures, in a self-righteous fantasy that he is good and they are evil. Since he has already accepted, forgiven, and valued his own Shadow, he can accept, forgive, and value the struggles others face in their own attempts to move beyond neurosis to wholeness.

Because he is so in touch with his inner world, the man accessing the Lover is able to withdraw a great many of his projections from others. He does not need to blame others in order to avoid blaming himself for his own dysfunctional psychic elements. Nor does he need to project his own strength, initiative, and potency onto others in order to avoid taking responsibility for these qualities in himself. Instead, he lovingly recalls all of who he is, in his strengths and in his weaknesses. He does not blame himself, or cooperate in the self-shaming he may have been taught as a child. He has compassion for his weaknesses and genuine appreciation for his strengths. He knows that what appears to be a weakness is often a hidden strength, and what appears to be a strength may disguise a hidden weakness.

The others he values and loves include his wife or lover, his parents, his children, his siblings, his friends, and his associates. In the end, he loves all human beings. But his concern and caring goes beyond the human race. He knows that he is bound to his brothers and sisters in the natural world—the waters, the land, the sky above, and the other animals and plants with whom he shares this planet. He is a man engaged in some form of community service. He contributes to some cause that furthers the well-being of humans, animals, or the larger environment, and he *takes actions* that demonstrate his concern for the ecosystem.

This man reaches out, emotionally and physically, to women. His feelings of amor are not discouraged by the destructive dynamics that intrude into all relationships between men and women. Rather, he works to minimize the destructiveness—or he takes action to extricate himself from a dead-end relationship. The amorous man will not accept a relationship that is nothing more than an uneasy truce.

The man appropriately accessing the Lover will also seek to bond with other men. He will learn to love, forgive, admire, and appreciate his own father. And he will compassionately value all of his male elders. He will come to understand why they have been absent emotionally or physically, how they themselves have been wounded, and why they might have attacked him. As an older man, he will minimize his feelings of fear and envy of younger men. He will embrace his sons, and he will realize how desperate young men are for his approval, his caring, and his blessing. He will become a nurturing ritual elder for them.

The man who is adequately accessing the archetypal Lover will extend his healing hand and embrace to others. He will take it upon himself to "heal the sick and cast out demons"[14] wherever and whenever he can. He will move to heal the suspicions and the fears that divide man from man, man from woman, nation from nation, and humankind from the ecosystem. He will work, through erotic, agapetic, and amorous feelings, to depotentiate the demons of hatred and rage that gather in the gloom of any space not illumined by love.

In his private life this man will seek to restore the lost Paradise of the Garden. As the gardener of his own small plot of ground, he will work, through love, to nurture and to grow rather than to cut off and destroy.

As Sam Keen and Erik Erikson have each pointed out, part of the business of living a life of generativity involves the rearing of children. The man appropriately accessing the Lover is likely to be a biological father. While the Lover's sexual enjoyment of eternal Paradise cannot be seen simply as an exercise in procreation, it remains true that the ultimate purpose of the erotic impulse is to ensure the survival of the species. More than survival is aimed at here. Part of the joy of loving is discovered by the generative man in teaching, in keeping safe, and in imparting a sense of adventure to his developing sons and daughters. He is motivated by the sheer joy of giving in order to enhance his children's prospects for greater self-fulfillment.

While not all men who are accessing the Lover adequately

The Lover as Generative Man: Caring for Future Generations

become biological fathers, all men who love involve themselves in *some* significant way with children. They may donate some of their time to youth programs in their communities, or become involved in professional counseling work with children, or work to stamp out drug use among teenagers in their neighborhoods. In these and in many other ways, men of all ages involve themselves in intergenerational love and caring.

They are men who are cultural innovators. Such a man, in whatever walk of life he finds himself, has a natural tendency to be open and receptive to new images, new ideas, and new methods. He is always an artist in a broad sense of the word. He is open to inspiration from the personal and collective unconscious. He will often receive intuitive solutions to problems in the middle of the night, or on the commute to work. He does not dismiss his intuitions. Instead he trusts that hunches and instincts issue from a deep and alert inner psychic space.

The man appropriately accessing the Lover supports structure—in the family, the corporation, the nation, the church, and the political party. But he demands that the structures he supports represent creative ordering, with the emphasis on "creative." Should he come to realize that these structures are more oppressive than liberating, this man may very well become a rebel, a whistle-blower, even a revolutionary.

The Lover ensures that the man who draws on his energies lives passionately. Such a man radiates a centered vitality and intensity. He is both content and free. His life pulsates with the strength of the phallus; he provides a fertile psychic medium for bringing others to life. In touch with the mysteries of life and death, he moves colorfully among all those with whom he comes into contact. He is awake in a world of sleepwalkers.

If he is free it is because he is not addicted. While he enjoys the pleasures of the senses, he does not become undone by them. He is not chemically addicted—to drugs, alcohol, tobacco, or any other substance. Nor is he addicted to his work or his relationships. He knows that he can live without any of these. He knows this because he has a spiritual perspective. He avoids idolatry—the investing of finite objects, events, institutions, or people with infinite meaning and potency. He chooses his own gods, but always keeps in mind that any god's particular path is only another path to the Garden. He knows that, while the Lover engages him in the process of incarnation, finally the archetype also points beyond the finite, temporal world to the infinite and the eternal.

If the man appropriately accessing the Lover bears a striking resemblance to the man appropriately accessing the King, the Warrior, or the Magician, it is because each archetype of mature masculinity interpenetrates the others. Each of the four archetypes requires the others in order to manifest its own full maturity. The man appropriately accessing one of the mature masculine archetypes is, in large part, accessing them all. A truly generative man is the result.

PART 3

THE UNINITIATED LOVER: MALFUNCTIONS AND SHADOW FORMS

7

THE IMPOTENT: LOST
IN THE WASTELAND

PERSONALITY DISORDERS INTERRELATE WITH ONE
another in a complex way.[1] They tend to fall primarily
into either passive or active categories, though these cannot be
neatly separated from one another. A man suffering from a
personality disorder will often move back and forth between
the active and passive categories. Also a man may exhibit
characteristics of any *number* of personality disorders at the
same time. While exceptions exist, disorders are often found
in predictable groupings. Thus the major personality disorders, and their consequent dysfunctional behavioral styles,
are often found in conjunction with one another.

The Grief of Impotence:
The Damned Soul
(Michelangelo)

We believe the dysfunctional bipolar Shadows of the major archetypes, as delineated in this series of books, underlie all personality disorders. Each bipolar Shadow system displays an active and a passive pole, either one of which may "possess" an Ego that lacks an adequate Ego-Self axis. Escalating pressures of one kind or another may cause the captive Ego's polarity to reverse—so that the Ego oscillates from one pole to the other.

We may find various diagnostic categories of personality disorders in the Shadows of the archetypes; some are more typical of one archetypal Shadow than of another. The passive pole of the Shadow Lover—the Impotent Lover—displays characteristics of the dependent, compulsive, schizoid, and avoidant personality disorders, as clinically defined.

THE LONGING FOR MOTHER

Robin Norwood's best-selling book, *Women Who Love Too Much*, details the phenomena of masochism, self-effacement, and exaggerated dependency issues among women. It is not widely recognized that many men face the same issues. If there is, on the part of many women, an unsatisfied longing for the perfect parent hidden in these symptoms, there is a parallel unsatisfied longing among men.

An interesting illustration of this may be found in Danny DeVito's blackly comedic film about divorce, *The War of the Roses*. Throughout the film, Michael Douglas's character, Mr. Rose, simply cannot come to terms with the idea that his wife, played by Kathleen Turner, no longer loves him. He continues to believe that they can settle their differences, and that he can cajole, charm, reason, or threaten her out of wanting to leave him. No matter what level of sadistic barbarity—emotional or physical—comes to rule the house that neither will relinquish, Douglas's character remains hopeful. In the final scene Turner and Douglas are both hanging from a chandelier. Its cable breaks. The cameras follow as the two hurtle to the marble floor far below. Turner and Douglas, their bodies twisted and broken in the wreckage, both open their eyes for a moment. With his last ounce of energy, Douglas reaches his hand over to Turner and touches her neck. With her last ounce of energy, she pushes his hand away.

A man's longing for the kind of mother he wanted, and his untiring pursuit of this feminine phantom—through marriages, affairs, and nasty divorces—reveals a deep childhood wounding as severe as that experienced by women who love "too much." The key to the masculine Impotent Lover lies in a certain critical period in boyhood, beginning with the birth trauma and continuing through the Oedipal Phase.

Boys must build a wall between themselves and their mothers in order to get the distance they need to experience themselves as fully masculine. The problem is that they are left with the impossible choice of either remaining feminine in order to stay in a human relationship—the only one they know at this early age—or breaking their feeling ties in order to become masculine.

The father plays the crucial role at this juncture. Unfortunately, most fathers, at least in modern Western societies, are absent emotionally, or physically, or both, most of the time. They are unavailable to their sons in this critical phase in a boy's psychological development. What the father needs to do at this point is to take his son to him, emotionally and physically, to hold him, to show him that he loves him. The boy needs to be reassured that he can depend on his father for relationship. Fathers need to nurture their sons in order to show them that while they do have to separate from their mothers in order to achieve a masculine identity, they do not have to forfeit warm and intimate relationship in the process.

Some other societies have been more successful in dealing with these developmental issues. One can walk the streets of the Orthodox quarter in modern Jerusalem, for instance, and see Hassidic fathers warmly relating to their sons. One can see the gleam of joy and approval, the light of blessing, in these men's eyes as they behold their young sons. And anthropologists have shown how tribal cultures go to great lengths to separate boys from their mothers at a certain time (usually in early puberty) and to *welcome* the boys into the realm of the fathers.[2]

If we add the dimension of the Oedipal conflict to the gender crisis most boys in our society face, we can see how their trauma is deepened. It may be that the Oedipal conflict manifests in the first place because of the lack of male nurturing available at the time of the gender crisis. Most mothers naturally want to cling to their babies. And most boys cannot bear to cut themselves off from the only deeply connected relationship they know. During the Oedipal drama, they turn back to their mothers at the very moment they begin to experience themselves becoming masculine. If no nurturing father steps in to take them by the hand and lead them away from the mother, these boys will become confused about their roles in the family. An unconscious dynamic will then urge them toward feelings of possessiveness toward their mothers. In the absence of a strong, wise, and loving father, the son will bond to his mother in an Oedipal way. This new bonding alienates the father, and leaves the boy feeling fearful, guilty, and deeply confused. He will be unable to develop a legitimate masculine identity in relationship to women.

As Robert Bly has pointed out, the problem with men in the United States is that they have not been able to separate from their mothers, because they have been unable to bond with their fathers. Men have been profoundly wounded in their inner Lover in ways that inhibit them from moving into mature masculinity. When they are unable to find a mature masculine way to love women, they remain immature lovers. They become "possessed" by the Oedipal Child. Chronic immaturity carries forward into the bipolar Shadow Lover in the "adult" man. Those men who fall under the passive spell of the Impotent Lover become emotionally depressed, paralyzed, and dependent. Those men who fall victim to the active pole of the Addict Lover become restless, histrionic, addicted, and overly "independent" (antisocial) as they seek to escape from being enmeshed in the sensual world. Oscillation between the passive and the active poles of the Shadow Lover is the rule, not the exception.

The Drooping Phallus
(*Soft Drainpipe*,
Claes Oldenburg)

IMPOTENCE

Emotional paralysis comes from the shock and the fear of having had our psychological boundaries invaded, of having been the recipients of emotional abuse, of having been rejected and abandoned in childhood, or of having been unable to break the "merger" with the mother. Impotence is its result. If we are raised by a mother who is an "inconstant love-object," who alternates offerings of love, nurturing, and affirmation with attacks, invasions, and criticisms, we learn to be on alert all the time. We learn to beware of the next "lightning bolt" which might fall unprovoked out of a blue sky.

With an inconstant, and thus dangerous and confusing, love-object, we develop a paralyzing ambivalence about our sense of self-worth, and even about the desirability of being in an intimate relationship. If we fall victim to the corrosive effects of chronic distrust, we also experience deep uncertainty about our borders—where we end and another begins.

Young children have few defensible borders. Their parents and older siblings are constantly "invading" their physical territory—the bedroom, for instance, or the bathroom. Enemas are administered to them, their pants are torn down before a spanking, vegetables are forced upon them, and in a host of other ways the message is conveyed that their room, their body, their physical space is not really theirs at all.

A young child's psychic territory is often similarly invaded. A psychological invasion is even more damaging than a physical one because it deprives the child of any sense of an autonomous and defensible self. Insensitive comments and directives from a more powerful other can cause a boy to split off and to repress whole aspects of himself in order to gain approval.

We've all heard parents say, to ourselves or to other children, "You don't really feel that way, honey." Such a comment denies the validity of a child's own feelings. Perhaps when a boy is fuming over some parental humiliation, he is told, "Give Mommy a kiss"; such a directive shames him further, and leaves him feeling guilty and confused about his anger. Perhaps the attack is more overt: "Get over here right this minute and wipe that smile off your face," or "I don't care if it hurts. Boys don't cry." So many boys in our culture, craving natural masculine affection, are scolded, "Shame on you for feeling that way toward your father!" A sexually repressed mother might tell her son, "Don't touch your penis. That's dirty!" Or, when a boy is engaged in creative play, "That's nonsense. Why don't you do something useful?"

A boy who is subjected to such invasions as these despairs

of feeling loved and celebrated for who he actually is. Chronic invasion of his psychological space leaves him carrying an intolerable weight of barely concealed rage. The rage is impotent because it cannot be acted out against his oppressors. It is seldom, if ever, realized, even in later life.

Beneath the rage is fear, not only of attack and criticism, but of an even more primal terror—annihilation. The other storms into the boy's inner world, as the Germans stormed into Poland. The boy becomes the victim of psychological terrorism. He cannot reach out to others, because the "other" for him means an annihilating "enemy." Interactions with those who get "too close" seem profoundly threatening to the fragile self-structures the boy has been able to construct between invasions. And yet, he *needs* to reach out to others, however inconstant they may be. The Lover requires it. The boy, indeed the man, who is caught between the titanic opposing urges to both enter into and defend against relationship, becomes emotionally paralyzed.

Vulnerability is not the virtue in human relationships that it is reputed to be. Receptiveness *is* a virtue. Sensitivity is a virtue. But a man who is deeply *vulnerable* may never achieve intimacy with another. Intimacy involves profound sharing between two selves, and a deeply vulnerable man has no bounded self to share. A vulnerable man is not accessing his inner Warrior. And without guards, there can be no Garden.

A man who cannot sustain an intimate relationship is likely to throw tantrums, and even to get violent. That doesn't mean his Warrior is developed. A man with a violent temper does not have a consolidated Warrior. With a consolidated Warrior, a man can control his infantile aggression and his temper. He can use his Warrior energy to protect the time he spends with his lover, and the space they need to be together.

A man in his late twenties, during a counseling session,

reported a recurring dream. He would dream he was lying in his bed at night, and just as he was nodding off, he would notice a cloud of "toxic, acidic fog" forming in the bedroom doorway. The cloud, becoming more and more palpable, would float into the room and rise to the ceiling directly above his bed. It would start to make "ghostly sounds." Fearing that he would be "dissolved" in the "acid," this man would wake himself up by growling like a dog and "baring his teeth" at the cloud. He had the distinct impression that the cloud was his mother invading his bedroom in a diabolic attempt to deprive him of his manhood.

Another young man, at the beginning of a new relationship, had a dream that dramatized the theme of emotional and phallic paralysis he was about to experience in this relationship, just as he had in all his previous relationships. In the dream, he got up in the middle of the night, went out into the kitchen, and opened the refrigerator. Hearing sizzling sounds coming from the freezer, he opened the freezer door. There, coiled up in the paralyzing cold and frost, ready to strike, was a huge snake, "sizzling and popping," red-hot with an inner heat. The snake was "stewing in its own juices," cooking "as if in a microwave." Yet it was unable to move. It was frozen in position. What better image for paralyzed Libido? What better symbol for the impotent phallus?

The man who is emotionally paralyzed, and who manifests phallic and libidinous impotence as a consequence, is a man who is deeply afraid. He is afraid to live out of his true Self, and afraid to reach out to others. Stunned by people's attacks upon him, he is unable to experience masculine joy, especially in the context of an intimate relationship. The young man who had the recurring dream of the "acidic fog" recalled that his mother had made him shave under his arms as a teenager, and then use her deodorant. As an adult, he married a woman who railed at him for having "too much" body hair and for "leaving" it on the bathroom floor. The man "possessed" by the Impotent Lover nearly always marries a critical, domineering woman who persecutes him just as his mother did. She shows the same disgust for his masculinity that his mother did. When his wife attacks him, often accusing him of slights against her, he is, like the frozen serpent, paralyzed with shock, fear, and repressed rage.

Such a man involves himself in relationships that compulsively recreate his childhood traumas. As Hendrix and others have argued, "repetition compulsion" aims ultimately at the working through of the original trauma in order to gain release from it. A man "possessed" by the Impotent Lover will continue to take the same kind of abuse he sustained as a child. His paralysis, vulnerability, and terror will actually invite escalating attacks from a mate.

Very soon his sex life will suffer. His Libido will diminish. His mate will notice, of course, and launch a new assault against whatever masculine structures he has left. She will accuse him of not desiring her, of not being capable of intimate relationship, of being interested in other women, or of other "crimes" against her. She will not realize that she has helped to constellate his impotence by her "bad mother" behavior toward him. As this new invasion begins, the impotent man descends into the misery of castration anxiety.

Fear and rage go together. As his fear and rage build, this man may exhibit obsessive/compulsive behaviors; these represent an attempt to defend against his devastating feelings. He may become compulsively tidy and neat. When he trims his moustache, for instance, he may immediately remove all traces of the cut hairs. He may start eating health foods, and working out three mornings a week at the health club. He may start watching every penny that he spends and take a more active interest in his investments. He may become a workaholic, further sublimating his Libido in a desperate attempt to substitute work for play.

These and other compulsive behaviors signal the growing pressure against the repression barrier of his unconscious passion and rage. He will build superficial structures to defend himself against the realization that he has no stable inner structure. He erects these neurotic fortifications against the threat of psychic invasion. But his false defenses will prove to be about as effective as the Polish cavalry proved to be against Hitler's Panzers.

Clinical and other evidence indicates that in order for a man to feel sexually alive he must feel reasonably safe from attack and invasion from the person with whom he is in an intimate relationship.[3] He must experience himself as strong and structured with legitimate and defensible boundaries. He must be able to say to his mate "this far, and no further." Unfortunately for the man possessed by the Impotent Lover, his struggle to defend and affirm his emotional boundaries is made more difficult by the mate he has with all probability chosen.

Like his mother, she will find it difficult to cooperate with his program of restructuring. His mother did not perceive her son to be anything more than an extension of her narcissistic needs, and she could not allow him to fully identify himself as masculine. She conveyed her own hostility toward men to her son, who learned that masculine identity and the masculine boundaries that identity entails are not legitimate, and are even shameful. Her son's wife or lover is likely to manifest a similar hostility toward his phallic joy, while at the same time demanding that he "perform" potently.

When the Ego that is possessed by the passive pole of the dysfunctional system begins to move toward the active pole, drawing closer as a consequence to the repression barrier, it falls into a depression. Depression, viewed from this perspective, is a self-administered anesthetic that keeps the Ego from experiencing underlying passion, fear, and rage. The man possessed by the Impotent Lover, rather than becoming agitated into potency by a woman's needling, will move from emotional and phallic paralysis into a dull affectless gloom. Elements of compulsive behavior may continue to manifest, but he will retreat further and further into the self-delusional "safety" depression affords him.

A depressed man exhibits signs of insensitivity and of emotional and sexual sterility. He lacks enthusiasm and vitality. He becomes "lackluster." His speech and tone of voice may become monotonous, demonstrating qualities of weariness and of defeat. He may lose his appetite for food, or find it hard to get up in the morning. A depressed man can even manifest dissociative phenomena, occasionally experiencing himself "outside" of his body, watching himself with bored disinterest. He may fall into the pathologies of the schizoid and the avoidant disorders.

A depressed man is often unable to "get it up." Even if he tries to will his penis to rise, it simply will not cooperate.[4] The boredom he may feel toward his mate and toward himself is an echo of the boredom his parents originally felt toward him. Rather than mirroring and affirming his erotic vitality, his parents displayed a profound disinterest in him. They blocked their own feelings toward him, and almost certainly toward each other as well.

When in adulthood this man reenters the wasteland of depression, cut off from his Libido, he will not be able to enjoy his body. He withdraws from the sensual world and its delights. At the same time, he withdraws from the spiritual realm. He despairs of ever recovering his primordial unity, his "polymorphous perversity," or his childhood world of intense feeling. He wanders far from the Garden of Delight and becomes lost in a pathless desert. He enters the land of the living dead. The unbounded ecstasy of the Lover in union with all things becomes the unbounded desert of the death instinct.

Masturbation is one way out of this wasteland of depression. Criticized in psychoanalytic literature as much as in the popular culture, masturbation is usually seen as an act of narcissistic self-involvement. It is certainly true that compulsive masturbation can carry a man away from sexual intimacy with flesh-and-blood partners. However, masturbation is also an act of self-soothing and self-affirmation. By masturbating, a man may invoke his phallic energy and his masculine joy. He may engage in a kind of "prayer" to the Lover within. Through masturbation, he can express a renewed hopefulness in the possibility of union with the feminine. In fact, he is achieving, however fragmentarily and fleetingly, some degree of union with the images of his own Anima—presented in his imagination or in the pages of pornographic material. Although, for the developmental reasons already cited, intimate relationship with actual women has proven "unsafe" for him, a man who compulsively masturbates is still affirming his desire to unite with the "other," even if that other is within his own psyche.

Masturbation may be a first step toward reaching out to real women (as it often is for children and for teenage boys), or, alternatively, it may be a "last-ditch" effort to shore up a dissolving sense of masculine potency; nonetheless there are problems with it. The man possessed by the Impotent Lover, once he has achieved climax, may feel self-castrated, or worse, ashamed and guilty. He will recognize on some level that he has failed to experience his masculinity in the fullness of its joy, which comes only in the context of sexual union with another. The tacit recognition of his failure to incarnate the Lover in the outer world may submerge this man in his sea of depression, and deepen his sense of isolation from others.

Often the impotent man will be drawn past his depression, and his only partially successful masturbatory attempts to feel his masculine joy, toward the repression barrier that separates the passive from the active pole of the Shadow

Lover. There this man may begin to evidence addictive behaviors. Addictive behaviors will already have manifested in the passive pole as defenses against depression, anxiety, and rage. They are always present, in some form, in the compulsive disorders that are a feature of the Impotent Lover. However, addictions are really incursions of the active pole of the Shadow Lover into the passive realm. At the repression barrier, the Ego reaches out for the other in idolatrous attachment, without overcoming the basic dependency issues or the yearning for "mother."

Our contemporary culture, in relationship to the Lover, is driven in two opposite directions. The dynamics of sublimation on the one hand, and of infantile acting-out on the other, drive men in our culture to both poles of the Shadow Lover. As a culture we are enslaved to the reality principle and to work, and opposed to the legitimate enjoyment of the pleasure principle and play. We move from a compulsive rejection of the values of the Lover, to the orgiastic acting out of sexual fantasies, and addiction to a seemingly endless variety of substances, fads, causes, and romantic attachments. Our age is as possessed by the Shadow Lover as it is by the Shadow King, the Shadow Warrior, and the Shadow Magician.

8

THE ADDICT:
POSSESSED BY
THE LOVER WITHIN

CERTAIN PERSONALITY DISORDERS MANIFEST characteristics of the *active* pole of the Shadow Lover, among them the histrionic and antisocial disorders. Histrionics[1] need to take center stage, to be the "life of the party," and to "charm" others into liking them. Their charm is facile and superficial; beneath a gregarious exterior lies a profound anxiety about self-worth, and often a sense of inner emptiness. As usual, when initial strategies for obtaining mirroring and love fail, and feelings of underlying terror and rage are too powerful to be experienced by the Ego, depression results. It is, as we have noted, a self-administered anesthetic.

"I Sought for Help, but No One Took Me by the Hand."
(Babylonian penitential psalm)

The Don Juan syndrome is an example of the histrionic disorder that barely conceals the repressed passive pole of the Impotent Lover. The antisocial personality[2] tries to assert an angry independence and "autonomy." This independence (from both societal norms and intimate personal relationships) is illusory. Beneath it lie significant dependency issues. Antisocial behavior often leads to various forms of addiction. Frequently, addictive behaviors begin as the flouting of an adult's—or the Superego's—authority.

Related to these problematic coping styles is the manic-depressive disorder, in which the psyche is caught alternating between ecstatic highs and miserable lows.[3] Manic-depressives tend to be exceptionally creative people, musicians particularly, although Van Gogh and Hemingway may also have suffered from this disorder. Containment and boundary issues typify the manic-depressive; he is unable to separate from or contain his powerful emotions. Manic-depressives often use cocaine, or other drugs, to artificially induce this high-low swing. This is one reason why drug use is so endemic among artists, who are especially connected with the Lover energy, in both its mature and immature forms.

The active-ambivalent disorder[4] oscillates between the poles of the Shadow Lover system. The active-ambivalent psyche is torn between dependency needs (the Impotent Lover) and a need to vehemently assert an autonomous identity (the Addict Lover).

Sadomasochism is another oscillating behavioral style.[5] Masochism is a feature of the passive pole, while sadism stems from the active pole. Since addictive behaviors are a kind of self-inflicted sadism, a masochistic bent can be observed in the active pole as well. However, sadomasochism, as we define it, is not primarily in the Shadow Lover's domain. It is related to love because of childhood dynamics in which the sadomasochist learned to associate eros with pain and suffering, but we believe it has more to do with power issues than with sexuality or with love. Therefore, we have already examined sadomasochism in some detail in the Warrior volume. Let us simply mention here that sadistic behavior against women is, fundamentally, the desperate attempt on the part of a weak masculine Ego-structure to detach from the feminine, and to affirm, with a brutality that reveals the degree of desperation involved, necessary boundaries and a sense of personal power.

The "Sin of Sensuality":
Enslaved to the Material World
(cocaine addict)

ADDICTION: "THE SIN OF SENSUALITY"

Only a strong Ego, with legitimate and viable boundaries, is capable of reaching out to another with love and concern, without feeling overly threatened and without losing a sense of itself. Because the Lover's drive toward union in sensual and sexual delight is such a powerful one, boundary issues remain problematic for the Lover energy, especially in its Shadow form. The Addict Lover begins by reaching out to the other. This is potentially much more than a narcissistic activity. This other is an object that gives him pleasure and joy. However, because the Addict Lover cannot readily hold his boundaries, he ends by surrendering his freedom and his sense of self to the enticing object, whatever that object may be. What begins as an act of independence reveals the underlying dependency issues.

If addiction begins in the active revolt of eros against work, and of antistructural pleasure against reality, it ends in a deeper enslavement of the Ego. It ends in the total surrender of individual freedom. The Ego possessed by the object of its love becomes obsessive-compulsive. It becomes functionally idolatrous. The drug, the food, the work, the person—whatever this captivating love-object is—becomes the Ego's god, the idol of its utmost devotion. This god—or demon—demands the surrender of more and more personal autonomy and psychological integrity. In extreme instances, the possessed man feels he must commit the most reprehensible crimes, even murder, in order to "feed" the god. In reaching out to the other in idolatrous love, the possessed man disappears into the other, and for all practical purposes ceases to exist.

Ecstatic disappearance into another is one dysfunctional path that Lover energy may take. Even among mystics, if annihilation of individual consciousness is the goal, we believe that the Shadow Lover is at work. The Lover in his fullness urges a man neither to narcissistic self-admiration nor to self-annihilation. Rather, the Lover inspires a man to simultaneously *affirm* and *transcend* his individuality. The question for the Lover is not "To be or not to be." Rather, it is *how* to be, in an enjoyable relationship with another.

The "sin of sensuality,"[6] as Reinhold Niebuhr calls it, is a sin against the Cosmic Lover who delights both in finite beings and in their interconnections. The sin of sensuality is the idolatrous attachment to a finite thing. Within such an attachment a finite thing is made to bear the significance and power that only "God" can legitimately carry. Within the psyche, the only valid object of the Ego's devotion and love is the Self. Attributing to any fragmentary aspect of the psyche, or the psyche's experience, the power and significance of the Self will result in major psychological dysfunctioning.

Much contemporary discussion of the problem of addictions uses a disease model. Alcoholism is regarded as a disease. Drug addiction is regarded as a disease. Now, eating disorders are regarded as diseases, as are sexual addictions, addictions to "messiness," to gambling, and to a host of other things. It is theorized that some addictions may be the result of chemical imbalances and genetic predispositions. At the same time, most theorists agree that while body chemistry may be a factor in addictive behavior, it is not the final, determining one. Psychological disorders (which are, of course, never wholly separate from biological ones) play the decisive role in determining who becomes an addict, and to what particular addiction he becomes enslaved.

Often our addictions, like our neuroses in general, manifest a highly symbolic quality. They point, poetically, to what is wrong in the addictive psyche, what is missing, and what needs to become more conscious.

Various forms of sexual addiction often point to inadequately incarnated phallic energy. The Don Juan syndrome, for example, is finally narcissistic. For all his histrionic machinations, a Don Juan is not *involved* with the women he seduces. If he does become involved with any one woman, because of his own developmental issues he will not be able to remain involved. He ends up compulsively chasing his Anima, with her promise of lasting ecstasy, from one woman to another. A Don Juan's addiction is to sexual ecstasy. In common with the other addictive types, he lacks the inner structure to be able to do what it takes to more fully incarnate the ecstasy he feels.

A Don Juan cannot build into this world, and into a real relationship in this world, the beauty and the joy he feels must be in the Garden. The Garden of Delight always seems out of

Addicted to Love: Don Juan

reach for him. This is tragic enough. But what deepens his tragic situation is that he becomes enslaved to a quick sexual "fix." His search for the Garden—which is really right under his nose, and not someplace else—becomes compulsive. He finds himself locked in an endlessly repeating cycle of ecstasy and disappointment. All of his farewells eventually heap upon him a burden of regret and grief which no mortal man can bear.

Eating disorders, too, reflect the addictive pattern. They

are always compulsive, and hence unconscious. Anorexia, in part at least, is an unconscious attempt to regress to the psychological and physical condition of early puberty, or perhaps even further back to an imagined asexual childhood. An anorexic feels inadequate to the tasks of adulthood, and worthless as a result. Where anorexia becomes a mortal condition, it may be a compulsion to disappear completely into the inorganic world, a world preexisting one's own conception.

Overeaters deal with similar feelings of inadequacy and worthlessness (and impotence) in an opposite way. The obese man may be possessed by childhood feelings of not being seen, and of not being taken seriously. He overeats, in part, in order to become "bigger," more significant, and in order to place himself in full view, where he cannot be overlooked. He may, along with these unconscious motives, also have the need to turn his body into a fortress of fat. This symbolic gesture is designed to affirm very considerable, if superficial and dysfunctional, personal boundaries. The obese man may wish to appear more threatening (like an enraged chimpanzee who "puffs" his size) in order to ward off attacks from the aggressors who invaded him in childhood, and whom he experiences "reincarnated" in his wife, children, friends, and associates.

There's an interesting bumper sticker that reads, "Fat People Make Better Lovers." While probably intended as an amusing and empowering bid for self-respect, the message reveals a deeper truth. Overeaters, like other addicts, are in close proximity to their Lover energy. If we lack ritual structures and we get close to an archetype, we're either going to be psychotic, or we're going to commit suicide. If we have to choose between addiction and suicide, an addiction will at least take longer to kill us.

A compulsive cigar smoker is a man whose sense of masculine potency may be shaky. He is attempting to experience his phallic passion. Freud was a heavy cigar smoker.

When accused, along the lines of his own theory, of needing to have a lit penis in his mouth all the time, he replied that "sometimes a cigar is just a cigar." This seems to be little more than a defensive retort. A cigar may be a cigar, but it is also an engorged phallus, one that burns with the fires of Libido. The cigar spreads an aroma of earthiness all around, "perfuming" the world with the animal smells of the instinctual Garden. What begins as a sensual delight, an encursion into the realm of Edenic masculinity, becomes in the end a compulsion.

One middle-aged man entered counseling ostensibly to get free of his cigar habit. He reported a story his mother had told him. This incident had occurred early in the course of his breast-feeding. Apparently, he had been a vigorous suckler, frequently bruising his mother's nipples. Once, during a particularly aggressive feeding, his mother was unable to bear the pain any longer. She violently pulled his mouth away from her breast. Blood spurted from her nipple with such force that it splattered the adjacent wall. She angrily vowed to wean her son immediately, and subsequently jammed the bottle into his hungry mouth whenever he cried.

All might still have gone well for the future cigar addict except that he soon developed a life-threatening allergy to cow's milk. This allergy left his body, as his mother later told him, "like raw beef steak." His agonized screaming exasperated her and drove a further wedge between mother and son, just at the critical time—the oral phase—when she most needed to mirror and celebrate her child.

Eventually, a milk was found that the boy could handle. But the damage was already done. The boy's ecstatic union with his mother had been violently interrupted, leaving him with an unfulfilled yearning for the archetypal Mother. In addition, what turned out to be a life-threatening poison had been substituted for his mother's life-giving milk.

This man's addiction to cigars not only was a way for him to affirm his phallus, it was also an unconscious drive to recapture an oral connection with a nurturing mother. More ominously, he was compulsively driven to repeat the trauma of sucking on poison. A feature of all oral addictions—whether to food, chocolates or other candies, alcohol, cigars, cigarettes, or other drugs—is the unconscious desire to ingest the narcissistic "supplies" that were interrupted and denied in the oral phase.

An alcoholic, as Jung long ago observed, symbolizes in his compulsive drinking of "spirits" his need to incorporate more of the Spirit.[7] Along with the self-soothing and anesthetizing aims of all addictions, an alcoholic is looking for an ecstatic, spiritual state of mind. Men who become alcoholics are missing a Dionysian dimension to their lives. They aren't just trying to "drown their sorrows." They're also trying to drink in the ecstatic delight and joy they should have been able to get from their parents. Deprived of such celebration in his childhood, an alcoholic man reaches out to the "other" in the bottle, hoping that it will value him, inspire him, and wake him up to the joy of life. As with all addictions, the opposite effect occurs. Alcoholic men become "dispirited." While the pleasure-giving substances of this world are in the Lover's domain, in the end only an inner connection with him is sustaining.

The founders of Alcoholics Anonymous sought Jung's advice as they planned their institution. They were able to develop one of the most effective ritual processes available in our contemporary society—far more effective than any process offered by most churches, for example. AA and related groups have been able to provide ritual and structure for individuals who grew up without either. As a result, theirs is the most serious death-defying spiritual discipline that we have.

Modern culture tends to pathologize ritual. Many men

will shy away from participating in any kind of spiritual practice, because of intellectual or philosophical objections. The
fact is, whatever our philosophy, there are psychological energies that can be usefully channeled through the use of ritual.
An addiction is itself a personal ritual. Whatever the physical
cost, the individual believes his addiction to be worth it—this
is one measure of how powerful the human need for ritual
structure is.

Cocaine addiction is one of the most widespread and
debilitating addictions of our time. It manifests, in common
with the other addictions, the drive to flee from the suffering
of this world into the "eternity of bliss" of the Garden. Still,
other factors may be even more significant. In the case of one
young man who entered a psychotherapeutic process to get
out from under his cocaine habit, it became apparent, during
the course of a number of sessions, that he was not talking
about how wonderful the drug made him feel. Instead he was
describing, at great length, how much he enjoyed staying up
all night with his male buddies, cutting the lines and neatly
arranging them on the tray. He described his delight in the
"ordeal," as he put it, of the all-night vigil, and in the "male
bonding" he felt. It was, he said, as if he were participating in
a secret and mysterious ritual that only men could share.

There are striking similarities between his descriptions of
the essence of his cocaine experience and the features of male
initiation rites among primitive peoples. He was encouraged to
do some reading on male secret societies, and on such Native
American religiocultural phenomena as the peyote cult, sweat
lodge ceremonies, and the rituals associated with the peace
pipe. In subsequent sessions, he reported his discoveries. The
significance of preparatory rituals for administering drugs
leading to out-of-body spiritual experiences, of ordeals, of se-
crecy, of male bonding, and of the importance of feeling initiated by other men were all discussed.

During the course of those sessions in which the psychospiritual significance of his cocaine rituals was discussed, this young man said that he felt a great hunger for the cocaine. On closer examination, it became clear to him that it wasn't the drug or its effects for which he was ultimately hungering. Rather, it was the whole complex of associated ritual elements. He was advised to discover for himself and implement meaningful alternative ritual practices. With the help of some of his "clean" male friends, he did exactly that. He reported that he felt free of his addiction in a relatively short period of time.

Addictions point to elements of the individual and collective psyche that have been repressed, and to developmental stages that have been interrupted. It is clear from this addict's experience that the absence in our culture of secret and ritual male bonding, and initiatory male organizations designed to convey the spiritual truths of masculine identity, is more damaging to the souls and to the physical health of men than has hitherto been noted.

LOST IN THE WORLD

It is not only in his addictions that a man possessed by the Addict Lover may become overidentified with the things of the sensual world. Such men may also become "lost" in a host of sensually approached love-objects. Painters get lost in their paintings, composers in their music, writers in their stories. One student of Hebrew had such a sensual approach to Hebrew words, the unusual shapes of their characters, and the alien worlds of images they conjured for him that he "short-circuited" and dropped out of his classes in emotional exhaustion.

Any of us can temporarily lose ourselves in the moods that sweep over us in response to a piece of music, a scene, or a news story. For especially sensitive men possessed by the

Addict Lover, becoming lost either in literal objects and processes, or in overly empathic feelings for the emotional states of other people, can be excruciatingly painful. Whenever we overidentify and overempathize with others, as ministers, as therapists, or simply as friends, parents, children, and lovers, we have forsaken our boundaries and our own psychological integrity. We then dance to a tune that another is playing, and we lose our wills. When this occurs, we cease to do ourselves or anyone else any good.

This "loss of soul," which primitive peoples experience quite literally as the soul abandoning the body, is often followed by physical death. One of the shaman's tasks, as we saw in the Magician volume, is to go after "lost souls" and return them to their owners, thereby averting their owners' deaths.[8] When we lose our souls in the world of things or feelings we are in danger of at least psychic death. Even in romantic love, the enchantment we may feel as we "give our hearts and our souls" to another is almost always an evil enchantment. The Libido-draining effects of such boundariless, addictive living are always, ultimately, self-destructive.

In the escalating feelings of desperation and hysteria that often accompany addictive and compulsive disorders, and in the repetition compulsions that characterize them, the psyche looks for a way out of its enchantment. The addicted man knows, at some level, that what originally seemed to hold the promise of freedom for him has come to be the agent of his enslavement, and possibly of his death. He oscillates between abstinence and binging, feeling himself sinking even more deeply into an emotional quicksand from which there is no escape.

He may start acting out in emotionally violent ways as he seeks to break free of his addiction. He may throw the bottle at the wall, slam the door on his wife and storm into the night, beat his children, quit his job, pitch out the whole box of

five-dollar cigars. He may go from obesity to being dangerously thin, and then back again. He may kick his cocaine habit
only to start drinking too much. He may stop smoking only to
gain an alarming amount of weight, trading the risk of lung
cancer for the risk of a heart attack.

As he becomes increasingly frightened and desperate, he
may find himself suddenly past the repression barrier and
possessed by the Impotent Lover. His unacknowledged feelings of dependency and his yearnings for an archetypal
mother and father will follow, leading to emotional paralysis
and a deep depression. Then, once again, his compulsive
behaviors and his old addictions, or new ones, will emerge.
Thus, the dysfunctional cycle of the bipolar Shadow Lover
continues until the Ego can get a "fix" on the archetypal Lover
in his fullness.

It is impossible to have a disordered Lover that does not
affect the other archetypes. An individual who gets erotic
gratification out of inflicting pain is a warrior whose Lover
energy is deeply out of balance. The warrior infused with
balanced Lover energy, on the other hand, is the man who
fights for worthy causes.

A "king" without Lover energy cannot bless and nurture
his people. He is a man whose drive for power outstrips every
other desire. With balanced Lover energy, a king can properly
care—in both senses, of stewarding and of adoring—for his
realm.

A magician who lacks a connection to the Lover is at
best a voyeur. Emotionally detached therapists are often
voyeuristic. They will rationalize their lack of caring, arguing
that "you shouldn't want to cure a patient. You don't want
to be too involved in his getting better. It's not professional." And it's certainly not profitable. When the Magician
operates in concert with the Lover, though, a mere diagnosti-
cian can be transformed into a healer. A healer cares enough

to suffer along with his patient, without, however, identify-
ing with him.

When a man apprehends the Lover in his fullness, he
embraces the liberating experience of being a finite and worthy self, intent on joyful *partnership* with another.

PART 4

EROTIC MAN: EMBODYING MASCULINE JOY

EMBODYING THE LOVER WITHIN

WHEN WE BEGIN APPROPRIATELY ACCESSING
the Lover we feel more alive than ever before. The
world seems to take on new color. We enjoy our lives in ways
we thought were lost with the passing of childhood. A deep
sense of authentic meaning fills our being. We feel our masculine joy and potency. We feel our personal and public lives are
romantic and filled with abundance.

Abundant life means different things for different men.
One man paints Mexican scenes in the earth tones and rainbow
colors that, for him, encompass this magic world. Another, on
his first Caribbean cruise, goes "skinny dipping" in the ocean

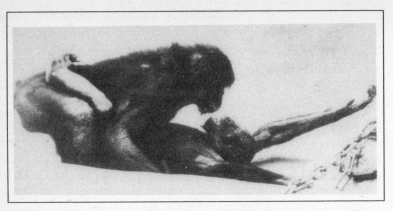

Face-to-Face: The Lover in an Intimate Relationship (bonobos at the
San Diego Zoo)

under the "mad moon" with the most beautiful woman on the
ship (who later becomes his wife). An architect dreams about
a fantastic skyscraper that looks like a layer cake, and then
goes out and builds it. A musician continues to believe, after
years of struggling, that he (like Orpheus) will find the one
musical phrase that will smite the hearts of all people and wake
them up to the beauty in each other.

*We can access the Lover within with the help of a variety
of imaging techniques—prayer, meditation, active imagination dialogue, dream interpretation, or a psychotherapeutic
process.* All of these techniques have been detailed in previous
volumes of this series. There are a number of additional techniques that apply specifically to the evocation of Lover energy.

*We suggest that every man schedule into each day of his
life at least one thing that he really enjoys*—one thing that
has nothing to do with his usual obligations, compulsions, or
"reality principle" activities. Whatever "play" means to you,
whatever gives you simple pleasure, we suggest you give yourself on a daily basis. This is an easy and immediate way for you

to love yourself. One man talks to his plants every day and waters and prunes them once a week. His plants respond and transform his apartment into a tropical paradise. Another man gets up early and sits in his living room, reveling in the sunlight that streams through his windows. Another mixes himself a chocolate milk every evening when he gets home from work, sipping it slowly, enjoying the rich taste and the smooth texture. Simple things such as these stimulate the senses and can leave us deeply satisfied.

There is a second, related technique that can help a man develop an "appreciative consciousness." At the beginning, *we simply need to feel the inner Lover's appreciation for sights and tastes and sounds.* We can come to appreciate the weather, to luxuriate in the smell and the feel of rain-heavy night air, the austere chill of a bracing wind, the mysterious tranquillity of snow falling, or the heat of the afternoon sun. We can listen to music from other cultures and learn to dance within ourselves to new melodies and rhythms. We can learn to delight in the forlorn look of an inner city alley, and the exotic accents of people on the street who come from unknown corners of the world. Instead of disliking intrusions into our worlds, we can welcome what are really opportunities to feel the richness and the diversity of life. If we tune ourselves to the frequency of sensual enjoyment, and open ourselves to positive appreciation of little things, our lives will never again be boring.

We can access the Lover, and through him the other, by learning to appreciate his most direct expressions in art. We can open our minds and hearts to the sensuality of forms, colors, brush strokes, and textures, as the great painters have used them. Our engaged appreciation of paintings need not be confined to any one school of art. We can embrace the paintings, for example, of the old masters, the Impressionists, the Fauvists, the Cubists, and the Abstract Expressionists. We can delight equally in the intricacy of Hindu sculpture, the smooth forms of Henry Moore's work, and the arresting inventiveness of Picasso's.

Our appreciation of art needs to extend beyond our feelings for other people's creations. A society that is accessing the Lover appropriately is a society of artists. On the island of Bali, because every boy is raised with a deep appreciation for art, *every* man is a painter, a sculptor, a musician, or a dancer. The Lover, as artist, is present in all of us, waiting for us to access his creative play. The feelings of self-satisfaction that come from creative engagement with our artistic impulses cannot be surpassed.[1] We suggest that every man engage in some form of creative play. You may perhaps learn to paint, or work with the potter's wheel. You may do the repair and remodeling projects on your home. You may indulge your desire to restore classic cars, or learn the art of gourmet cooking. Whatever creative projects you undertake, you will, in the process, be expressing and celebrating the Lover.

As a further step in the embodied meeting with the other, we suggest that a man learn to dance. By dancing, he will come to know his own body more fully, and meet the other in body as well as soul. So many of us forget that we have bodies, except when they fall ill. The man appropriately accessing the Lover always feels his body and experiences it as an instrument of pleasure. There is dancing associated with almost every popular music, and we must follow wherever our personal taste leads us.

The lover-king of the ancient Hebrews, King David, danced in naked ecstasy before the Ark of the Lord. A lot of religious groups suppress dancing, because they recognize how quickly dancing puts people in touch with their Lover energy. When rock and roll became popular, there was a wholesale invocation of a fairly primal Lover, hence all the attempts to suppress the music.

The Lover as Cosmic
Dancer: Shiva Dancing
(south Indian)

A man need not be ashamed to appear, nor to fill up all of his space. Dancing is closely related to display. As a man grows comfortable moving and being in his body, he'll become more interested in clothes and fashion. The current state of male fashion says a lot about the state of men's inner Lovers in this society. If a man has no interest in how he dresses, it's obvious where he is hurt. He has a lot of shame issues. Dressing up doesn't have to cost much—and it's one immediate way to bring the Lover into your life.

The man seeking to access the Lover in his fullness can

meet the other in the world of ideas. He may come to love learning. He may embrace ideas, turning them over and over in his appreciating mind and heart as if they were real things. In reality, that is exactly what they are. They are the things of the human psyche, things that ultimately manifest more trans-formational force than any of the more tangible objects of the material world. A man may come to feel the texture of ideas, envision them, and taste their flavored nuances. And in so doing, he may follow the lead of the artist and incarnate some of these ideas through action in the world.

We suggest that a man wishing to access the Lover seek to develop his capacities for mystical experience. He may visit what are to him especially beautiful sites, a lakefront, or a field. One man says that he enters a "mystical state of mind" whenever he flies. He experiences a sense of anticipation of something momentous as the plane leaves the earth. Once in the air, detached from the world below, he realizes that his fate is not in his own hands. With that he relaxes his Ego and allows his Spirit to soar. He begins to feel at one with the vast world spread out below him, and with what he calls the "Spirit in the sky." He falls into a state of mystical reverie identical to that of the ancient magicians and shamans who experienced their psychospiritual adventures as "flights" into the heavens where the Creator dwells in eternal peace and grandeur.

The man seeking mystical encounters may do so through attending religious services, if those services impart to him a genuine sense of mystery and cause him to meditate upon the sensual beauty of the spiritual dimension. On his own, he may meditate upon images of aesthetic beauty that communicate to him the presence of the mystical Lover.

Finally he can meet the other by engaging in the Lover's work in the world. He can become active in a cause or a project that expresses love and appreciation for other human beings, for other species of life, or for the environment as a whole. At the very least, he can do some of the simple things to "save the earth" that are now being suggested by various environmental publications and by the news media. In a more intensive way, he may support, through gifts of time and money, human and animal rights organizations, and environmentalist groups. Without the passion of the Lover we will be unsuccessful in our struggle for healing engagement with the ecosphere.

CELEBRATING SELF AND OTHER
IN RELATIONSHIP

In the end, if we are to access the Lover adequately and appropriately, there is no substitute for an intimate relationship with another. Jung said that the "individuation process" can take place only in the context of such a relationship.[2] He used the alchemical images of the Red King and the White Queen, and their union in conjunction, to illustrate what he meant. Joseph Campbell has described marriage as the coming together of two parts in order to make a transcendent whole, a whole which then takes on a life of its own.

Romantic love presents us with an opportunity for embodied meeting, though with several attendant dangers—of idolatry, and of the chronic disappointment of our ecstatic impulses.

Robert Johnson writes in *We: Understanding the Psychology of Romantic Love* of his Jungian approach to the "cult of romantic love."[3] Johnson uses the Tristan and Iseult legend to explore the dimensions of this issue. In the end, Johnson takes a dim view of the romantic impulse in human relationships. He notes the impossibility of any human being carrying the romantic projections of another. Romance, says Johnson, is fundamentally a spiritual phenomenon, and the

The Night of
Scheherazade
(Marc Chagall)

legitimate objects of its devotion reside in the collective unconscious.

But through romantic involvement with a woman, the
Lover is seeking to connect a man with his Anima, and
through this relationship to the archetypal Self, or "God."
From a psychological perspective, what we seek from romantic
love is union with lost elements of our own psyches and the
transhuman realities that lie behind them. For Johnson, our
amorous longings can never find their satisfaction in human
relationships. We can find our "bliss" only through an inner

psychological connection with the archetypes of the collective unconscious, and, ultimately, with the Self. Romantic love is, therefore, misdirected spirituality. What human relationships are for, according to Johnson, is compatible friendship. They are for the amicable sharing of humble tasks and activities.

In his short book *Ecstasy*, Johnson elaborates a Dionysian spiritual vision, and spells out the methods we can use to connect ourselves to an inner paradise. He shows us how we can begin to move our spiritual impulses away from our human relationships and toward the imaginal realm within.

While we agree to a large extent with Johnson's analysis of the problems associated with romantic love, his conclusions are not satisfying. He splits off the ecstasy of embodied encounter with the other entirely into the psychological or spiritual realm. Thus he furthers the mind/body split which is so characteristic of Western civilization. Like a Gnostic or a Manichean, Johnson advocates a disincarnate Spirit. Ecstasy, for him, must be left to the imagination, and cannot be embodied in time and space. The Garden of Delight cannot be brought into this world, and the Lover must remain a psycho-spiritual entity only realized in the context of what we would label narcissistic self-involvement. He cannot be legitimately experienced in embodied meeting with a flesh-and-blood other.

As we have seen, Harville Hendrix takes a similar yet ultimately different tack. Hendrix believes that the feelings associated with "falling in love" are, in part at least, the result of the psyche's experience of its own lost elements in its relationship with the beloved. The person we fall in love with displays repressed aspects of our own personalities. The ecstasy we feel as we encounter the "other" in embodied meeting stems from the profound joy of feeling whole again. The Lover within evaluates potential lovers and mates on the basis of how well their apparent characteristics fit the parental Imago. If the match is exact enough, especially in terms of the negative characteristics of our parents, then we "fall in love."

Hendrix's analysis of romantic love explains why most relationships turn sour. Our ecstasy subsides as we begin to recognize that another person cannot, as we had hoped, do the work for us of an inner psychological reunion. We have to integrate the lost parts of ourselves on our own. Our disappointment turns into downright panic as the inner Child sees that the other is going to wound it in exactly the same ways as the parents did. We soon realize that getting the love we want from this kind of person is not going to be an easy thing. It is at this point that former lovers become enemies and proceed to a power struggle that leaves most partners ready either to kill each other or to flee the relationship.

This is also the point at which many couples separate or file for divorce. The problem with this, Hendrix believes, is that once a wounding other is gone from the scene, the inner Child will begin scanning all over again—for the same kind of person. Repetition compulsion will drive us into relationships with the same kinds of mates until either we can get the love we want from them, through mutual transformation, or we despair about love entirely and settle for an uneasy and unfulfilling "truce." In what Hendrix calls the "parallel marriage," which the vast majority of "stable" marriages become, each person goes his or her own separate way, seeking joy and love outside of the marriage—in work, friendships, children, or affairs.

Hendrix believes that the enemy stage of intimate relationship can be worked through. In fact, he says, it must be worked through in order for both partners' inner Children to be healed. He elaborates a number of exercises the partners can do, some separately and some together, for getting the love they want from each other. And he concludes his book with a vision of relationship that he calls "passionate friendship."

Hendrix has much of interest to say about the problems and promises of romantic love. While we believe that his analysis of why we fall in love is largely correct, we think that the apparent lack of an authentic spiritual dimension in his thought, together with his lack of familiarity with the Jungian archetypal perspective, has seriously hampered his approach.

In the first place, we believe that the inner Child's longing for perfect mirroring and affirmation is based only partly on his damaged relationship with his parents. His desires are for far more than "mother" or "father"—his desire for amorous union arises from a genetically inherited "wiring." This wiring disposes us to wish for union with the Self, with "God." We yearn for the perfect parent because we have inherited knowledge of an essential, ideal Parent. We yearn for the Garden of Delight beyond the Wall of Paradise because we have been there. We long for infinite satisfaction because we have known it. Thus Johnson is right to say that no human relationship can ever provide us with all of the love we ultimately want. We want infinite love because we have known it through the collective unconscious, in the "Kingdom of Heaven."

Any project or therapeutic process that offers us the hope of embodying bliss completely within the context of our personal relationships is holding out a false promise. Or at least it is taking too mundane a view of the Lover's ultimate aim. Such a process does not understand our instinctual wiring. It has not grasped the implications of the Jungian phenomenology of the Self, and of the archetypal foundations of human feeling, thinking, and behaving. Ultimately, the ecstasy Hendrix analyzes is much tamer than that which Johnson knows, and which all great artists and mystics have known.

Perhaps Hendrix is radically incarnational without having an adequate grasp of what he wishes to incarnate. If Johnson maintains the traditional split between mind and body, Hendrix effectively collapses the spiritual into the mundane. Both Johnson and Hendrix minimize the sensual and sexual expression of the Lover in human relationships. Johnson opts for a spiritual-ized eros, and Hendrix envisions agape "rescuing" eros.

A man appropriately accessing the Lover companions his beloved in mutual and ecstatic friendship. This ecstatic friend-ship embodies all the dimensions of love, but especially amor. *We* believe that our intimate relationships, at their best, serve to open gates in the Garden Wall. Once through these gates our bodies incarnate the Spirit of Love, which dwells at the center of the Garden. Our souls, through the sensual and sexual delights of the body, disincarnate and become one with that Spirit. In our relationships, we need, each for the other, to push aside the Gatekeeper's "fiery sword," which blocks the way back into the Garden. We can do this partly through the process Hendrix describes, of healing each other's inner Child. And we can do this partly through a Jungian rapproche-ment between the Ego and the imaginal realm of the collective unconscious.

We believe that it is appropriate for us to expect our intimate relationships to further these Edenic tasks. With all due attention to our own wounding, we nonetheless have a primordial responsibility to refuse to accept quiet desperation as a substitute for truly joyful relatedness. Mutual and ecstatic friendship lies in the simultaneous experience of the other as other and of the self as self (in the affirmation of mutual boundaries) *and* of ourselves and the other as one.

As we find ourselves, through love, consolidating our relationships with our Anima and with those "others" within who need our love and celebration, we also find ourselves consolidating our relationships with those others, and that special other, in our "outer" lives who need our love and our celebration. Thus, we become joyously, tenderly, exuberantly phallic men. We become truly generative men, for ourselves and our own lives, and for all those others who share this garden planet with us.

EPILOGUE:

JOY TO THE WORLD: RETURNING TO THE GARDEN THROUGH LOVE

T HE REASON THAT WE CAN TOLERATE ALL THE horror we impose upon each other and upon other species of life on this planet is that we are cut off from the Lover in his Garden. A Shadow has fallen between the creative Word, which is spoken with infinite Love, and the world of time and space. Expelled from Paradise, we have lost our depth. The "dance of Maya" intervenes and Brahman seems to forget who and what he is. The Lover is exiled to the realm of forgotten Childhood, and we labor "by the sweat of our brows" in an atmosphere of scarcity. The good, the delightful, the pleasurable, and the playful all seem to be in short supply.

The Cosmic Lover: Compassion for All Things
(*The Savior*, Pedro Berruguete, 1501)

We become lost in a hell C. S. Lewis imagined—where a man sits on the ground, unable to see the blessings of God raining down upon him. He dies of thirst, not knowing he could simply stretch out his cupped hand to receive the "waters of life."

When the Lover comes, everyone and everything is revalued. A cloud of ignorance is suddenly lifted and all people are beheld and known as being all of the same royal house. The Lover pronounces the ultimate Word of Love—he says, "What you have done unto the least of these, you have done unto me."[1] He does not say, "What you have done unto the least of these, it's *as if* you have done it unto me." He says, "The Kingdom of Heaven is within you."[2]

When the Lover comes, he comes manifesting signs "in heaven and on the earth."[3] The skies open. Angelic beings sing the hymns of universal goodwill. Wise men bow their heads in worship, and the poor and oppressed laugh for joy. When the Lover comes, the lion and the lamb lie down in peace together; the innocent boy plays unafraid with his phallic power.[4] The Lover builds an Ark, embraces all living things, saves them from the wrathful storm, and begins Creation anew.

When the Lover comes, east and west, north and south are seen as one celebrated whole. Diversity and unity are known as two sides of the same golden coin. High and low, physical and spiritual, man and woman, death and life, all come together and embrace under the Gate to the Garden of Delight. *Valuing leads to generative action.* What has always been is recreated.

We, and all things with us, are incarnations of the Lover. When the Lover comes, he says, "Lift the stone and you shall find me; cleave the wood and I'll be there."[5]

May your embodiment of the Lover bring joy to yourself and to your world!

Appendices

APPENDIX A

DECODING
THE QUATERNIO:
BEYOND JUNG

IN THE FOLLOWING BRIEF DISCUSSION WE WILL discuss how we have furthered Jung's work on the deep structure of the Self. Our work builds upon his fundamental metapsychological assumptions.

Many Jungians have forgotten the nature and depth of Jung's commitment to the *quaternio* and *double quaternio* structures of the human Self. Jung believed that the human preoccupation with quadration reflected a structural reality in the collective unconscious. His best-known work on quadration is his typology—particularly in his explication of the four functions of intuition, thinking, feeling, and sensation. Less well known is his idea that the totality of the archetypal Self has been imaged clearly in the octahedron.

He presented his most extensive exposition of this double quaternio of the deep Self in his essay "The Structure and Dynamics of the Self" in *Aion*. Jung's intent was to articulate the various ways in which an octahedral shape of the Self may be shown to contain psychological insight (fig. 1). While he struggles mightily to make his case, many have found his exposition hopelessly opaque.

A few prominent Jungians have continued to search for the key to Jung's fascination with this particular octahedron. Others have adopted a similar octahedral shape to explain the deep Self, but have reinterpreted the meanings of the diamond's various facets and planes. Notable among these is John Layard's exegesis in *A Celtic Quest* (fig. 2). Layard suggests that an analysis of Celtic mythology leads to an octahedron that locates the archetypal Self in the lower pyramid and the human individuating Ego in the upper. The archetypal feminine joins the Self below. While somewhat more intelligible than Jung's study, Layard's ingenious interpretation of the diamond body has not become widely known for any clinical usefulness.

One more useful schema has been offered by Toni Wolff. In her essay *Structural Forms of the Feminine Psyche*, Wolff demonstrated how a feminine quadration could be seen to be expressed by more than typological distinctions (fig. 3). She delineates the four major feminine structures as the Mother, the Amazon, the Medial woman, and the Hetaira. Her work comes closest to anticipating our structural decoding, though her model has certain limitations. For a more thorough study of these, see Appendix C. Suffice it to say here that while she correctly sees these four forms to be important feminine structures, she misses their underlying archetypal dimension. In our terminology these dimensions are described as the Queen,

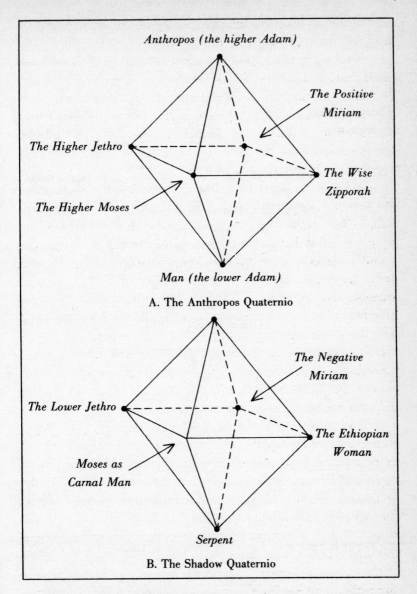

Figure 1: From Carl Jung, "The Structure and Dynamics of the Self" in *Aion*, Volume 9, Part 2 of the *Collected Works*, p. 231.

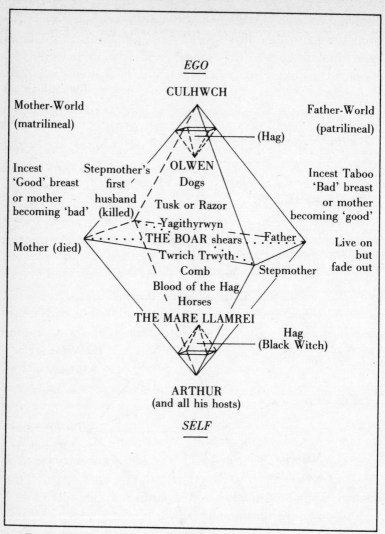

Figure 2: From John Layard, *A Celtic Quest* (Dallas: Spring 1975),
p. 202.

Warrior, Lover, and Magician. Wolff discerns aspects of the archetypes but describes for the most part traits of the feminine bipolar Shadows. Her model omits a necessary emphasis on balancing these four aspects in the movement toward individuation. Also she seems unable to interpret the dialectics that she correctly observes to exist between the Mother and the Medial woman, the Amazon and the Hetaira.

Ironically we investigated these other models only after constructing our own. We did not approach this topic deductively, fitting psychological data into an a priori octahedral structure. Rather we came to the double pyramid model inductively, seeking to understand the shape our research findings seemed to be urging. Later we were astounded and gratified to find that others had struggled to decode the same diamond body.

Our model (fig. 4) has grown out of over twenty years of anthropological field research and clinical psychoanalytic research. If you examine this model carefully, you will note the two fundamental dialectical oppositions built into the psyche's deep structure. These are between eros and aggression (the Lover and the Warrior), and ruler and sage (the King/Queen and the Magician). Freud focused of course on the eros/aggression dialectic, and Adler on the ruler/sage (cf. his work on superiority and social interest). Thus Jung was not entirely correct to ascribe Freud and Adler's conflict purely to typological differences. The two were focusing on different structural dynamics inherent in the deep structure of the Self.

We believe the human predilection for fourfold structures is grounded in an intuition of an inner quaternio. Each quadrant represents in a way a distinct "program" encoded with psychological potentials necessary to a cohesive and fully functioning human Self. The King program contains the ordering and nurturing potentials. The Warrior program holds potentials for boundary foundation and maintenance, effective

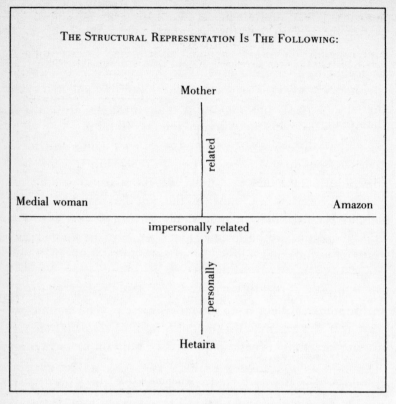

Figure 3: From Toni Wolff, *Structural Forms of the Feminine Psyche* (Zurich: C. G. Jung Institute, 1956), p. 4.

organization, action, vocation, and fidelity. With the Magician program lie potentials for cognitive functioning, understanding, death, and rebirth. Receptiveness, affiliation, healthy dependency, embodied sexuality, empathy, and intimacy are all potentials characteristic of the Lover program.

Each of these programs must be adequately accessed, then balanced one against another in a healthy dynamic tension, analogous to the tension of a well-functioning human

DECODING THE DIAMOND BODY: THE DEEP STRUCTURES OF THE
HUMAN SELF

1. Models of the engendered self in quadrated form (the quaternios)

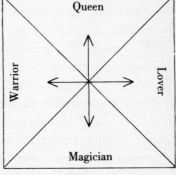

The masculine self   The feminine self

Arrows above indicate dialectical tensions built into the deep
structure of the psyche

2. Models of the complete bisexual Archetypal Self in octahedral
form (the double quaternio)

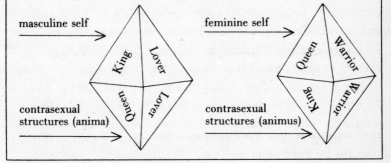

Figure 4: From Robert L. Moore, *The Magician and the Analyst:
Ritual, Sacred Space, and Psychotherapy* (Chicago: Center for the
Scientific Study of Religion, 1991).

musculature. Individuation and wholeness are not just eso-
teric concepts. The psyche has clear and discernible components available to it that require deliberate sustained efforts to
be attained, consolidated, and maintained. On the basis of our
model, individuation requires development along four axes.
This development counteracts the dialectical tensions built
into psychic structure.

We chose the pyramid for our model because it most
graphically illustrates the struggle involved in individuation.
Wholeness is imaged in the capstone of the pyramid. From
the eye of illumination printed on our one-dollar bill to the
temple on top of the Mayan pyramids, we have noticed the
support mythological traditions give to our intuited model
of the goal of psychological and spiritual quest. We believe
we have been privileged to stumble, in the course of our
researches, across the actual psychological structure underlying these mythic images.

While the relation of the four foundational archetypes to
Jung's theory of typology has yet to be researched, there does
not seem to be any one-to-one correspondence. It seems likely
that we will find sensation and feeling in the Lover's quadrant,
and intuition and thinking in the Magician's—but typological
theory neglects the other two of the four quarters. Jung's
insistence that Shadow work precede deep work on the Anima/
Animus is, we think, clearly imaged in our model. Here the
contrasexual is a realm as rich and diverse as that of the
engendered Ego—yet deeper in the psyche and more difficult
to understand.

Finally we think our model helps make sense of the way
in which male and female developmental challenges are similar—in the four powers there are to be accessed and integrated—and different—in their structural organization. This
structural asymmetry will, we conjecture, help us understand
gender differences in developmental trajectories, psychopa-

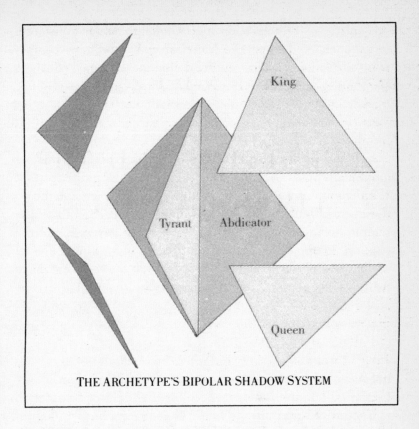

THE ARCHETYPE'S BIPOLAR SHADOW SYSTEM

thology distributions, and perceptual and communication styles. In short it seems Jung did in fact intuit the biomorphic form of the psyche's deep structures. We believe our model is a decoding of that structure, enabling us to relate together research data from many different sources, and confirming Jung's assumption that the psyche is structured as an octahedral double quaternio.

APPENDIX B

ARCHETYPES AND THE
LIMBIC SYSTEM

ACCORDING TO A NUMBER OF BRAIN RESEARCH-ers, most notably Paul MacLean, the limbic system (augmenting the more basic instincts of the underlying R-complex, or reptilian brain) is the seat of mammalian and species-typical instincts for all primates, including humans. Located in the paleocortical area, the limbic system consists of the fornix, hippocampus, cingulate cortex, anterior thalamic nucleus, amygdala, septum, the mammillary bodies, and associated hypothalamic areas. The paleocortex (as the term's Greek roots suggest) is the older brain, a region we share with other mammals. Ours is genetically configured particularly like the paleocortices of other primates.

Because the mechanism of evolution serves to develop new structures gradually, based upon older ones, there remain in our bodies any number of archaic structures that continue to fulfill their more primitive functions. One familiar vestigial organ, the appendix, no longer serves any apparent function (it is believed to have once aided the digestion of grasses) and because of this is now a frequent site of infection. The limbic system, however, continues in its inherited functions, and suggestively seems to be the locus for foundational archetypal structures—suggestively because this would appear to link human archetypes with the instinctive patterns of other species.

Paul Broca, in 1878, was the first to identify a large convolution common to the brains of all mammals as the "great limbic lobe."[1] In 1937 James Papez realized that this limbic system was the seat of the experience and expression of emotion.[2] Paul MacLean later developed the full concept of the limbic system.[3] MacLean came to believe the system was not only the center for emotion but also the integration center for correlating "every form of internal and external perception." It has, he claims, "many strong connections with the hypothalamus for discharging its impression."[4] While some researchers do not accept this notion, there appears to be no other neurological system available to play such an integrative role.

Within the limbic system are three primary subsystems:

1. the affiliative/attachment subsystem[5]

2. the autonomy/aggression subsystem[6]

3. the integrative/inhibition subsystem[7]

The affiliation/attachment subsystem, as the name implies, is almost certainly responsible for general mammalian tendencies to form social units characterized by nurturing, affection, and play. In humans and other primates these affiliative impulses may result in such complex psychological and social phenomena as reliance, dependence, and collaboration. The affiliative impulse seems to arise (along with each specie's particular structures of affiliation) primarily in the cingulate gyrus.[8] MacLean has proposed that the concept of "family," for example, may be structured into the limbic system.[9]

Exploration, fear, defensive strategies, fighting, the acquisition of territory, the need for control (over the inner and outer worlds), and other self-definitive, self-preservative behaviors are a result of the autonomy/aggression instinct. This impulse enables humans to form cohesive selves through adversity. It may also give rise to the instinct to order society hierarchically.[10] The autonomy/aggression subsystem appears to be located in the amygdaloid complex.[11] There is evidence that in primates the amygdala plays a hierarchically ordering role for our societies.[12]

The third major limbic subsystem mediates the integration/inhibition instinct and is apparently located in the hippocampus and the septum.[13] MacLean believes this subsystem is the integrative center for the entire nervous system.[14] The hippocampus can be thought of as the gatekeeper of the limbic system, which system is the capital of the nervous system as a whole. Teamed with the neocortex (which brings cognitive functions into play), the hippocampus "gate mechanism" seems to be responsible for regulating, arranging, prioritizing, and modulating data from nearly every aspect of the nervous system. The hippocampus regulates alternating affiliative/attachment and autonomous/aggressive behaviors. When properly operating, this system regulates these competing drives to appropriately interact with any set of environmental stimuli, both inner and outer.

We believe that the four foundational archetypes we present in this series arise in the limbic system and are then elaborated and refined as they pass upward through the neo-

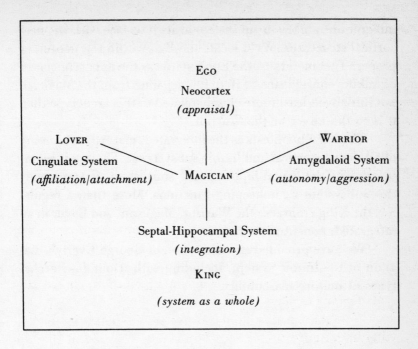

cortex. This elaboration may be primarily achieved either by the Left Brain's rational, logical functions, or by the Right Brain's intuitive, holistic mode. They may be given "humane" form especially in the frontal lobes, which seem to be responsible for empathetic and altruistic emotions as well as for refined cognitive processes. In order for the Ego to know and access any of the four major archetypes, it must experience a particular archetype as an asymmetrical composite of each of the others. In light of the brain research we've cited, a provocative correspondence suggests itself between the archetypal and the limbic systems.

It seems clear that what we call the Lover arises originally in the affiliative/attachment subsystem, and our Warrior arises in the autonomy/aggression subsystem. The Magician (which some other psychologies mistake as the Ego) arises in the

integration/inhibition subsystem at its interface with the neocortical structures. We'd locate the Ego within the neocortex
proper. This maintains the Ego's status as the apparent center
of waking consciousness. Here it is separate from the Magician
but initially at least more closely related to this archetype than
it is to the Lover or the Warrior.

The King manifests as the integrated, mature functioning
of all the neocortical and limbic subsystems. Though it seems
to arise in the septal-hippocampal subsystem, it transcends
this subsystem's gatekeeping functions. More than a regula-
tor, the King embraces the Warrior, Magician, and Lover in an
integrated, constitutive manner.

We have provided an elaboration of George Everly's diagram of the limbic system, including with it our four archetypes of mature masculinity.

APPENDIX C

ARCHETYPES AND THE ANIMA

I N THIS APPENDIX WE WILL SKETCH OUT SOME OF the structures and dynamics of the feminine psyche. Our particular interest will be in the Anima, the inner feminine element of the masculine psyche. We follow Jung in emphasizing that Shadow integration must precede serious work with the contra-sexual Anima or Animus. Implicit in Jung's approach is his understanding that integration of the personal Shadow solidifies the integrity of the Ego, and its achievement of a healthy psychosexual identity. Without a cohesive nuclear self, work with inner contrasexual structures can be confusing at best, and dangerous at worst.

We add to Jung's insights a description of the actual structural configurations of the contra-sexual Anima. The structure is similar for the feminine Animus (the inner masculine subpersonality in a woman), as we will make plain. As we've argued, the Shadow system involves both a personal Shadow and the bipolar Shadow of each of the four archetypes. After attending to the initiatory and integrative processes involved in mastering this Shadow system, a man can safely turn his attention to his Anima.

The aim of a relationship with the contra-sexual should not be to develop androgyny. Androgynous personalities entertain grandiose fantasies of "completeness within the Self." While there may be some genuinely biologically based androgynous personalities, as some brain research seems to suggest, for most men and women, androgyny is a masturbatory narcissistic stance, a kind of psychological hermaphroditism. For most people, any attempt to join the contra-sexual to the Ego results in a regressive merger rather than a mature complementary relationship. A merger with the Anima renders a man incapable of forming a mature relationship with his inner feminine energies, as surely as it skews his outer-world relationships with women. Jung believed that as a man's Ego grows stronger, his awareness of the contra-sexual as truly "other" will increase, until finally he can initiate what should become a lifelong relationship with his personified Anima through dreamwork, active imagination, and any other techniques he finds useful.

Contrary to what some contemporary Jungians claim, we believe the Anima is not an amorphous, ethereal "mood." The Anima has a dynamic structure that mirrors that of the masculine archetypes. As our diagram on page 234 (explicated in Appendix A) illustrates, the Anima is the feminine inverse of the four-faceted masculine archetypal pyramid. Turned upside down, the model becomes that of a feminine psyche. A

Lover). The Queen, however, provides images of all of these traits.

Wolff's second mistake is to weight the feminine Warrior with the culturally compromised image of the Amazon. In our system, the feminine Warrior is clearly related to Wolff's Amazon, but the legendary Greek form she's chosen often misdirects the aggressive energy that is this archetype's domain. Instead of using this energy in the service of the royal couple, supporting and extending the created cosmos, the Amazon of the myths all too frequently uses her aggression against males, even to the point of exiling her sons.

The fully expressed feminine Warrior helps a woman consolidate an independent Self by defining and defending legitimate psychological boundaries. The Warrior enables a woman to achieve other difficult tasks through strategic thinking, self-discipline, and hard work. But the feminine Warrior is not in any sense antimale. The Warrior does not misinterpret the battles she must fight as narrow tribal disputes, except in the legitimate defense of a woman's offspring. Where her children are threatened, a woman accessing her Warrior is programmed to react with swift and relentless ruthlessness. Otherwise, the woman in an axis with her Warrior correctly sees her battles as primarily personal efforts to establish a Self, and as transpersonal efforts to defend creation.

But by using the largely negative image of the Amazon, Wolff ends up really examining primarily the Shadow Warrior, in her sadistic expression. Possessed by the Sadist, a woman's fury is directed not only against men in general but against other women as well, and even against her own children.[1] A woman who allows the Amazonian Sadist to act for her in her life misses the potential benefits of the full expression of the feminine Warrior.

We hope the resources of the feminine Warrior will be accepted more fully into our culture. We would then see women engaged in a more active psychological and physical defense of themselves and their mates, as well as a fuller participation in the struggle against communal and global forces of destruction. There is evidence that our culture is increasingly learning to steward this energy—especially in the arenas of social and environmental reform.

The Hetaira is, like the Amazon, a culture-bound term. In ancient Greece the Hetaira functioned much as the more familiar geisha did in Japanese culture—as a well-educated female companion and prostitute. But a prostitute is a manifestation of the Shadow Lover, no matter how well-educated. In Wolff's system the Hetaira displays both aspects of the Lover's bipolar Shadow, the Addict and the Impotent Lover. The Addict is operative in Wolff's claim that women under the influence of the Hetaira have a tendency to go from one man to another. The Impotent Lover is disclosed by the knowledge that psychologically a prostitute is often engaged in a fruitless repetition of her unsuccessful childhood attempt to gain her father's admiration and love.

The Hetaira seems to be a second-generation archetype, composed of fragments of more basic ones. She includes both poles of the Magician's Shadow—as a Manipulator she causes a woman to use men for their money and her own narrow interests, and as the Innocent One she lures a woman into displaying her naïveté about relationships. The Sadist manifests in a woman's underlying anger toward men. The Warrior's other Shadow pole, the Masochist, appears in her willingness to place herself in harm's way.

To the extent Wolff's final type, the Medial, approaches the concept of the shaman, it is an appropriate and full expression of the archetype of the Magician. It is Wolff's least limiting term.

Despite any other shortcomings, it is striking that Wolff's conceptualization of the archetypal dynamics of the *feminine* psyche agrees so closely with our own system of thought concerning the *male* psyche. We interpret this as a verification of our instinct to extend the concept of the quadrates psyche from the masculine to the feminine Self, and to the Anima and Animus.

To our way of thinking then, a woman's quadrated psyche functions just as does a man's She balances the energies of four foundational archetypes—the Queen, Warrior, Magician, and Lover. The Queen guides a woman toward a centered calm, a sense of inner order she can extend into the outer world. She becomes gifted with the capacity to bless and join in fructifying union with the other members of her "realm." The Warrior guides a woman in self-discipline and self-defense, as well as in the defense of others. Her achievements are encouraged by the Warrior, and her sense of service to a Transpersonal Other reinforced. The Magician provides a capacity to introspect, to raise and contain power, to heal and to act as a mediator between the human and the divine spheres. Drawing on the Magician's powers, a woman may serve as a spiritual guide to others, especially in the task of initiating younger women into the mysteries of adult responsibilities and joys. And the Lover empowers a woman to be passionately and creatively engaged with all things, to be uninhibited sexually (playing and displaying) and profoundly spiritual.

Of course, the relationship between the masculine and feminine aspects of the Self are often problematic. For the Anima is a whole structure, and no man experiences it simply piece by piece, pair by pair. Just as he balances the energies of *his* four foundational archetypes, he must balance the four different signals that reach him from his Anima. It can be useful to separate out the different sources of these signals in order to distinguish their characteristics, so long as we remember that they operate as a whole.

The feminine energies beside each of the male archetypes

give them depth and definition. But when a man is caught in one or more of the bipolar Shadow systems of the masculine archetype, he encounters *all* of the Anima's complementary Shadow energies too. At the Warrior's *active* Sadist pole, for example, he will meet with the *passive* poles of the Shadow Anima, the Weakling/Abdicator, the Innocent One, the Impotent Lover, and especially with the Masochist. If he is Ego-identified instead with the Masochist, he will be confronted by the feminine Tyrant, the Manipulator, the Addict, and especially with the woman Warrior at her Sadist pole.

Relations between the masculine and feminine Warriors can be particularly strained. The only really successful mode for a relationship between them is as comrades-in-arms.[2] Otherwise the aggressive/aversive energies they each channel can be directed against the other, causing empathic breaks in man-woman relationships that are difficult to repair. A Warrior needs an enemy, and too often the masculine and feminine Warriors make enemies of each other.

A man who does not access the fully expressed Warrior (whose feminine counterpart is his comrade-in-arms) will tend to experience his Anima, and all the women in his life, in a split and shadowy way. He will see one aspect of the feminine as the Tyrant Queen—his sophomorically idealized and "virginal" mother. Women who are not like her he sees as whores, and we've seen what a complex mixture of Shadow elements a prostitute carries. The Tyrant Queen sends this man to his death to defend her. He, in turn, "fucks" a whore (rather than "making love" with her) in an act of revenge against his mother, overcoming "her" resistance with brutality. Here is the power issue the rapist fails to manage. He wants power over what he sees as an inordinately powerful, abusive woman. Perhaps his mother was physically or verbally abusive to him, or perhaps she was neglectful and uninterested. Such a man is of course not accessing his Warrior appropriately. Instead, he is a psychotic boy without any experience of his legitimate power.

Until a man becomes secure in his masculine identity, he will remain a sadomasochist in his relationships with women. If he is not secure he feels that he is risking invasion by his Anima. He has yet to learn to respect his own legitimate territories as well as those of the feminine psyche, both within and without. The maturing male learns there is a space within him he can never invade, and that will never be "his." He must approach his Anima with respect. Once he learns to deal with this "other" with discipline and respect, he has the prerequisite knowledge necessary to deal respectfully with any "other," including the women he loves, other men, other species, and finally the Transpersonal Other we all need to serve.

The octahedral Self we diagrammed in Appendix A gives a good visual model for imagining these Anima dynamics. While it does not portray the vital interpenetration of the masculine and feminine structures, it does show how the contra-sexual system is contained *within* the total structure, and is in no way external to it. The two structures together form the "diamond body" of the great Self. Though it is in some sense merely a pictorial construct, it is an appropriately suggestive and allusive one. Like the implicit structure of a crystal, we each have a perfect diamond Self within, waiting the chance to form. We are gifted then with an inner vision of the possible human which has the clarity, radiance, and perfection of a jewel.

NOTES

Complete bibliographical information on works cited in these notes will be found in the Bibliography that follows.

CHAPTER 1: GENDER IDENTITY, GENDER ASYMMETRY, AND THE SEXUAL IMBALANCE OF POWER

1. By "radical androgyny" we refer to the claims made by some feminists, whether male or female, that there are no differences between the sexes (except what they regard as incidental biological divergences). When it comes to assigning blame, however, particularly for

aggressive behavior and fear of intimacy, some feminists draw very clear distinctions between the sexes, always at the expense of the male. One would think from their claims that women have no Shadow. A woman's only weakness seems to be that she "loves men too much." It is impossible to love someone too much. What *is* possible is to become so addicted to another that personal responsibilities are relinquished. However, shadowy business of this kind is common to both sexes. The idealization of androgyny is against nature and scientific evidence; it is also hypocritical. For related discussion, see Robert Ardrey, in toto but especially *African Genesis*, pp. 143ff. (in Bibliography under Anthropology); James Ashbrook, *The Human Mind and the Mind of God*, pp. 57–59, 96–97, 105, 322ff., 324–327, 339 (in Bibliography under Brain Research); Sam Keen, *Fire in the Belly*, pp. 195ff. (in Bibliography under Other Psychologies); Anne Moir and David Jessel, *Brain Sex: The Real Difference Between Men and Women* (in Bibliography under The Lover, the Forms of Love, and Relationship); Anthony Stevens, *Archetypes: A Natural History of the Self*, pp. 23ff., 48ff., 81–84, 174ff. (in Bibliography under Jungian Thought); Edward O. Wilson, in toto but especially *On Human Nature*, pp. 16, 18–21, 121ff. (in Bibliography under The Lover, the Forms of Love, and Relationship).

2. An example of this phenomenon is Riane Eisler, *The Chalice and the Blade: Our History, Our Future* (in Bibliography under Anthropology). Although Ms. Eisler purports to demonstrate a "partnership" model of male/female relationships, she provides a stereotypic negative metaphor of the "Blade" to designate male qualities. Her central image of partnership is of a mother Goddess nurturing her child, by implication her son—hardly a relationship between equals. Also see Mary Daley, *Beyond God the Father and Gyn/Ecology*; and Rosemary Ruether, *Sexism and God-Talk: Toward a Feminist Theology*, pp. 104ff. (both in Bibliography under Theology and Philosophy).

3. Alice Miller, *The Drama of the Gifted Child*, *For Your Own Good*, and *Thou Shalt Not Be Aware* (in Bibliography under Other Psychologies).

4. Research in this area clearly links the development of high civilization (beyond the "high culture" of the late Neolithic) with the advent of sacral kingships and the attendant assemblage of larger nation-states. For an extensive record of sources, see the Bibliography's Kingship listing. See there especially Basham; Emery; Frank-

fort, *The Birth of Civilization in the Near East;* Kwanten; Schele and
Freidel; and Wales. See also Julian Jaynes, *The Origin of Conscious-
ness in the Breakdown of the Bicameral Mind* (in Bibliography under
Brain Research); John Weir Perry, *Lord of the Four Quarters* (in
Bibliography under Mythology and Religion); and Wilson, pp. 89–90.

5. Carl Jung, *Aion* in *The Portable Jung*, pp. 148ff.; Jolande
Jacobi, *The Psychology of C. G. Jung*, pp. 5, 114ff., 120–121; Carl
Jung, *Man and His Symbols*, pp. 186ff., and *Mysterium Coniunctio-
nis*, and Stevens, pp. 174ff., 193–194 (all in Bibliography under Jung-
ian Thought); Loren Pedersen, *Dark Hearts* and John Sanford, *The
Invisible Partners* (in Bibliography under The Lover, the Forms of
Love, and Relationship).

6. Moir and Jessel, p. 31.

7. Stevens, pp. 79–80; and Wilson, pp. 132–137.

8. See Bibliography under Brain Research.

9. David Gilmore, *Manhood in the Making: Cultural Concepts
of Masculinity*, "Work" in the index (in Bibliography under Anthropology).

10. Don Browning, *Generative Man*, p. 145ff. (in Bibliography
under Other Psychologies).

11. Niebuhr isn't always as frank about his distrust of power as
Lord Acton was when he said, "Power corrupts, absolute power corrupts absolutely." He does frequently, however, cast the desire for
power, and its achievement and uses, in an exaggeratedly negative
light. He assumes (as liberal Christians have for centuries, and some
feminists do today) that the quest for power is inherently mistaken,
and that its achievement is invariably destructive for principal and
subordinate alike. Writers such as Keen, Ruether, Eisler, and Daley
betray an unconscious utopianism in their works—and as Stevens
notes in *Archetypes* (p. 139), utopianism will always fail.

12. Gérard Lauzun, *Sigmund Freud: The Man and His Theories*,
pp. 64–65 (in Bibliography under Other Psychologies); and Reinhold
Niebuhr, *The Nature and Destiny of Man*, pp. 44, 192 (in Bibliography under Theology and Philosophy).

13. Anthony Stevens, *The Roots of War*, pp. 36–38 (in Bibliography under Jungian Thought); and Anthony Storr, in toto and especially *Human Destructiveness*, pp. 11, 21, 23, 34, 42 (in Bibliography
under Other Psychologies). Even Gilmore affirms the almost universal
necessity for aggressive male behaviors, as channeled into the cultur-

ally defined roles of protector, provider, and procreator. Keen finds himself (pp. 112ff.) endorsing "fierce gentlemen" as if they were vital to the survival of the species. This comes after his emphatic rejection of sociobiological claims and the notion of an aggressive instinct, and despite his embrasure of the romantic socialization model of gender definition.

14. Cultures have seldom celebrated initiation ceremonies for their girls. By and large girls have been considered naturally initiated by their first menstruation. Boys have been, in contrast, forcibly taken through initiation rituals designed to awaken in them an awareness of their risk-taking and self-sacrificial responsibilities. This may also reflect a widespread human awareness that innate masculine aggressive potentials require extremely careful containment and channeling if they are not to become dangerous to the human community in the behavior of irresponsible, immature, "monster boy" males. See the Bibliography under Ritual and Initiation; see also Mircea Eliade, *Rites and Symbols of Initiation* (in Bibliography under Mythology and Religion); Gilmore; Joseph Henderson, *Thresholds of Initiation* (in Bibliography under Mythology and Religion); Keen, pp. 27–33; Victor Turner, *The Ritual Process: Structure and Anti-Structure* (in Bibliography under Anthropology); and Hutton Webster, *Primitive Secret Societies* (in Bibliography under Anthropology).

CHAPTER 2: DECODING THE MALE PSYCHE

1. See Bibliography under Jungian Thought.

2. Carl Jung, "The Relations of the Ego and the Unconscious," in *The Portable Jung*, p. 75; Jolande Jacobi, *The Psychology of C. G. Jung*, p. 1; Aniela Jaffé, *The Myth of Meaning: Jung and the Expansion of Consciousness*, pp. 40–42; Carl Jung, *Psychology and Alchemy*, p. 215; and Anthony Stevens, *Archetypes: A Natural History of the Self*, pp. 43–47 (all in Bibliography under Jungian Thought).

3. Jacobi, *Psychology of C. G. Jung*, p. 1; and Stevens, *Archetypes*, pp. 43–47.

4. Joseph Campbell, *The Hero with a Thousand Faces*, pp. 3ff. (in Bibliography under Mythology and Religion); and Jacobi, *Psychology of C. G. Jung*, "Mythology/Myths" in the index.

5. Campbell, *The Hero with a Thousand Faces*, p. 258.

6. Mircea Eliade, *Cosmos and History: The Myth of the Eternal Return*, p. 3 (in Bibliography under Mythology and Religion); Jacobi, *Psychology of C. G. Jung*, pp. 5–10; see the first two chapters on the nature of consciousness in Julian Jaynes, *The Origin of Consciousness in the Breakdown of the Bicameral Mind* (in Bibliography under Brain Research); and Henri Frankfort, *Kingship and the Gods*, pp. 27–29 (in Bibliography under Kingship).

7. Carl Jung, "Aion," in *Psyche and Symbol*, pp. 1–6 (in Bibliography under Jungian Thought).

8. John O. Beahrs, *Unity and Multiplicity*, especially chs. 1 and 4 (in Bibliography under Other Psychologies).

9. Nearly every school of psychology acknowledges this, in one way or another. The Jungian approach to the Shadow, the work of developmental psychologists with the inner Child (see especially Alice Miller), and the work of hypnotherapists like Dr. John Beahrs with multiple-personality disorders all are particularly relevant.

10. Carl Jung, "The Structure and Dynamics of the Psyche," in *The Portable Jung*, especially p. 52; and Stevens, *Archetypes*, especially pp. 26, 40, 51ff.

11. Carl Jung, "The Concept of the Collective Unconscious," in *The Portable Jung*, pp. 59–69.

12. Bruno Bettelheim, *Freud and Man's Soul*, pp. 53–64; and Gérard Lauzun, *Sigmund Freud: The Man and His Theories*, "Id" in the index (both in Bibliography under Other Psychologies).

13. Don Browning, *Generative Man: Psychoanalytic Perspectives*, p. 158 (in Bibliography under Other Psychologies).

14. Ibid.

15. Ibid., p. 159.

16. Ibid., pp. 145–147, 158, 159; Jacobi, *Psychology of C. G. Jung*, "Libido" in the index; and Lauzun, *Sigmund Freud*, "Libido" in the index.

17. See Bibliography. Although Jean Bolen does not do this, she tends to identify the Gods and Goddesses with human personality types. Bolen's Gods and Goddesses do parallel cognition, feeling, and behavioral styles observable in men and women. *But no human being is an archetype, and neither is any God or Goddess.* Bolen's work describes complex configurations of archetypes (our foundational four from the psyches of men and women, as well as countless others that determine our modes of perception) as expressed through different

Ego identities, personal complexes, cultural and Superego conditioning, etc. Her Gods and Goddesses are simpler than human personalities, and so on this level they approach the archetypes more nearly than all but the most dysfunctional human personalities. But we believe the Libido takes form at the most basic levels of drive as either a King (or Queen), Warrior, Magician, or Lover, and then after progressive explication and diversification presents itself in complex manifestations. These foundational four are the node around which collect the culture-specific ideals, parental introjects, and other family myths that provide so many layers of archetypal functioning.

18. Jacobi, *Psychology of C. G. Jung*, pp. 1–9ff.

19. Marie Louise von Franz, *Projection and Re-Collection in Jungian Psychology*, "Shadow, Projection of" in the index (in Bibliography under Jungian Thought).

20. Individuation is a matter, for Jungians, of bringing into Ego consciousness (1) what has been otherwise split off and repressed, as well as (2) awakening insights that have never been conscious. For the distinction between complexes and archetypes, and their relation to the two categories above, see Jolande Jacobi's *Complex, Archetype, Symbol in the Psychology of C. G. Jung* (in Bibliography under Jungian Thought).

21. See Theodore Millon's excellent work with the concept of bipolarity in *Modern Psychopathology* (in Bibliography under Other Psychologies).

22. Theodore Millon, *Disorders of Personality: DSM-III: Axis II*, in toto but especially p. 58 (in Bibliography under Other Psychologies).

23. James Hillman et al., *Puer Papers*, especially Hillman's chapter "Senex and Puer: An Aspect of the Historical and Psychological Present" (in Bibliography under Jungian Thought).

24. Paul Tillich, *Systematic Theology*, vol. 3, especially ch. 1 and "The Kingdom of God as the End of History" (in Bibliography under Theology and Philosophy).

25. Ibid., "Hegel" in the index; also see Sean Kelly, *Individuation and the Absolute: Hegel, Jung, and the Path Toward Wholeness* (in Bibliography under Theology and Philosophy).

26. See Bibliography under Theology and Philosophy; see also Alfred North Whitehead, *Process and Reality* (in Bibliography under Theology and Philosophy).

27. Jung, *Psychology and Alchemy*, "Coniunctio" in the index.

28. In Greek mythology and legend, the Symplegades were two great rocks in the middle of the ocean. When a ship tried to pass between them, they would rush together and destroy the ship.

29. Stevens, *Archetypes*, pp. 259–275.

30. Ibid., pp. 260, 264. For the relevance of the limbic system to the four foundational archetypes, see Appendix B.

31. Rudolf Otto, *The Idea of the Holy*, in toto but especially pp. 12ff., 25 (in Bibliography under Mythology and Religion).

32. Eliade, *Cosmos and History*, pp. 12ff., and Eliade, *Patterns in Comparative Religion*, "Temple," "Tree, Cosmic," "Palace," "Mountain, Cosmic" in the index (in Bibliography under Mythology and Religion).

33. Eliade, *Patterns in Comparative Religion*, "Kings," "Rulers," in the index. The literature on sacral kingship, and the king's mediation of the sacred and profane worlds, is vast. See also the Bibliography under Kingship.

34. See Bibliography under Kingship. Also see James Frazer, *The Golden Bough*, "King," "Queen," in the index (in Bibliography under Mythology and Religion); and John Weir Perry, *Lord of the Four Quarters*, p. 32 (in Bibliography under Mythology and Religion).

35. Jane Goodall, *In the Shadow of Man*, p. 284 (in Bibliography under Primate Ethology).

36. Jane Goodall, *Through a Window*, p. 13 (in Bibliography under Primate Ethology).

37. See Bibliography under Primate Ethology. Also see Frans de Waal, *Chimpanzee Politics* (in Bibliography under Primate Ethology); Goodall, *Through a Window* and *In the Shadow of Man*; and Michael MacKinnon, *The Ape Within Us* (in Bibliography under Anthropology).

38. Geoffrey Bourne, *Primate Odyssey*, pp. 321ff. (in Bibliography under Primate Ethology).

39. de Wall, *Chimpanzee Politics*, "Alpha Male" in the index; and Goodall, *In the Shadow of Man*, pp. 112ff.

40. de Waal, *Chimpanzee Politics*, pp. 109–110, 200, 204–205.

41. Goodall, *In the Shadow of Man*, pp. 73–74; MacKinnon, *The Ape Within Us*, p. 85.

CHAPTER 3: THE GARDEN, THE PHALLUS, AND LIBIDO

1. See, for example, the Koran (56:1:56), excerpted in Alden Williams, *Islam* (in Bibliography under Mythology and Religion).

2. The image of the cross as the Tree of Life and of Christ as the Fruit of Eternal Life appears in Christian art and mysticism throughout the early period and the Middle Ages. See Mircea Eliade's lengthy discussion of the Tree of Life image in world mythology in *Patterns of Comparative Religion*, "Tree" in the index (in Bibliography under Mythology and Religion); also Edward Edinger, *Ego and Archetype*, "Christ" in the index (in Bibliography under Jungian Thought).

3. The image of Libido as the "Waters of Life" is found throughout world mythology. Sometimes these Waters are seen as divine milk issuing from the Goddess' breasts, and at other times as divine semen. See Edinger, *Ego and Archetype*, "Water of Life" in the index; and Eliade, *Patterns in Comparative Religion*, "Water" in the index.

4. This, of course, is a biblical image for the uniting of opposites in a new/old creation—in effect, a return to the Garden of Eden (Isa. 11:6, 65:25).

5. A Moslem image for the union of the masculine and feminine in a state of bliss. See, for example, Manoocher Aryanpur's rendering of *The Rubáiyát of Omar Khayyám* (in the Bibliography under Literature).

6. See Joseph Campbell, *The Masks of God: Creative Mythology*, p. 168 (in Bibliography under Mythology and Religion).

7. In some Jewish and Christian mystical traditions, including that of Irenaeus, Adam and Eve lived a blissful, if nonsexual, life before they awakened to the duality of good and evil. They were at one with each other, at least in a spiritual if not sexual sense. Some mystics imply, though, that their union was sexual as well.

8. For delightful translations of several ancient Egyptian love songs, see in Torgny Säve-Söderbergh, *Pharoahs and Mortals*, the chapter entitled "In the Shade of the Sycamores: Of Perfumes and Love" (in Bibliography under History).

9. This is the great realization of what can be called "spiritualized eros," the goal of Hindu tantric practices. It can be argued that sublimated eros is the real force behind all of those mystical systems of

thought and experience that grasp or are grasped by the sense of the ultimate identity of all things—for example, the Hinduism of *The Upanishads*, aspects of Jewish Kaballah, Moslem Sufism, the Platonic and Plotinic systems, and the Christian mysticism of Boehm, Cusa, and others. (See general works in Bibliography under Mythology and Religion, and Theology and Philosophy.)

10. See Henri Frankfort, *Kingship and the Gods*, "Seth" in the index (in Bibliography under Kingship).

11. 1 Cor. 15:54–55.

12. Physicists speculate that the four forces that have set the parameters of space and time, prior to the Big Bang that inaugurated our universe, were one. According to the most recent speculations, that oneness existed in what has been termed the Planck Era, after the great physicist Max Planck. It is thought that the Planck Era was character- ized by a kind of bubbling foam in a dimension entirely different from the one we know. See in the Time-Life series *Voyage Through the Universe, The Cosmos*, pp. 104–105, for a discussion of the Planck Era (in Bibliography under Physics and Cosmology).

13. The Jungian literature on Shadow-integration is enormous. But see, for example, Jolande Jacobi's discussion in *The Psychology of C. G. Jung*, pp. 109ff, and Carl Jung's essay "The Phenomenology of the Self" in *The Portable Jung*, ed. Joseph Campbell, pp. 144ff (both in Bibliography under Jungian Thought).

14. Again, the literature about the Anima and the Divine Child is vast. For quick reference, see *The Portable Jung*, pp. 148ff. For a first look at the archetype of the Divine Child in the psyche, see Carl Jung, *Aion*, pp. 31 and 195 (in Bibliography under Jungian Thought).

15. Matt. 18:2–5, 19:13–15; Mark 10:15; Luke 18:17; and John 8:3,5,7.

16. Sigmund Freud's term for the nongenitally focused sexuality of prepubescent children. The term *perverse* here does not strictly mean "abnormal," except in the sense that Freud believed that mature sexuality was genitally focused.

17. See Barbara Hannah, *Jung: His Life and Work*, pp. 195–196 (in Bibliography under Jungian Thought).

18. Hindu mythology is, when taken as a whole, profoundly *un*- systematic, so that masculine and feminine creative principles arise from each other and then turn back toward each other and fertilize each other, thus creating the world. The ultimate Creator is generally

thought of as either masculine or androgynous (see Mythology and Religion, and Theology and Philosophy in the Bibliography).

19. Campbell, *The Masks of God*, p. 226. Also see Robert Graves, *The Greek Myths*, vol. 1, p. 106 (in Bibliography under Mythology and Religion).

20. See Jean Bolen, *Gods in Everyman: A New Psychology of Men's Lives and Loves* (in Bibliography under Jungian Thought).

21. This is because damage to our budding self-structures early in life, especially in the period of "primary narcissism" when we need to be let gradually down off our "thrones," causes us to fixate at childish levels of development. We get stuck because we have not been enabled to grow, at least not in a healthy way, beyond our unresolved, phase-specific issues. Indeed, adult self-structures may be erected around and above the damaged sectors of the child's self-structures. But these adult structures will always remain vulnerable and tend to at least temporarily collapse under pressure to the extent that the self-structures of the child within have not been solidified. Under the surface of our adult interactions, then, the wounded child continues to clamor for recognition and healing, and, consequently, a part of us remains fixated. When our flimsily constructed adult self-structures crumble under pressure, we experience a regression to the level of the damaged child. Only to the extent that we can both heal *and* learn to contain the child within are we able to proceed to vigorous accessing of the archetypes of adulthood in life-enhancing ways. See Robert Moore and Douglas Gillette, *King, Warrior, Magician, Lover: Rediscovering the Archetypes of Mature Masculinity*, for an overview of this psychic situation (in Bibliography under Jungian Thought).

22. See Don Browning, *Generative Man*, especially ch. 3 (in Bibliography under Other Psychologies).

23. See Browning, *Generative Man*, "Marcuse, Herbert" in the index. Also see Herbert Marcuse, *Eros and Civilization*, "Nirvana principle" in the index (both in Bibliography under The Lover, the Forms of Love, and Relationship).

24. The "Essence of Mind" is a Buddhist concept of a form of consciousness that is simultaneously deeper and higher than our usual Ego-consciousness. See Browning's discussion of Norman O. Brown's notion of the convergence of the life and death instincts in "nirvana," *Generative Man*, pp. 69–70.

25. Seeing the world in a grain of sand is, at its root, a state of

mind urged upon us by many of the world's mystic traditions, and it is essentially a realization of the holographic nature of the universe. That is to say that the whole is contained in each of its parts. Even modern physicists and cosmologists are lifting up this mystical intuition in a scientific way. See, for example, David Loye, *The Sphinx and the Rainbow: Brain, Mind and Future Vision* (in Bibliography under Theology and Philosophy). See also William Blake, *Auguries of Innocence* (in Bibliography under Literature).

26. See C. S. Lewis, *The Four Loves* (in Bibliography under Literature).

27. This seems to be the import of a number of Jesus' sayings, for example, in Luke 16:8–9.

28. See G. S. Kirk and J. E. Raven, *The Presocratic Philosophers*, "Empedocles" and "Parmenides" in the index (in Bibliography under Theology and Philosophy).

29. See James Moffatt, *Love in the New Testament*, p. 37 (in Bibliography under The Lover, the Forms of Love, and Relationship).

30. See Plato's "Symposium" in Benjamin Jowett and Louise Ropes Loomis, eds., *Plato* (in Bibliography under Theology and Philosophy).

31. See Moffatt, *Love in the New Testament*, pp. 37–38.

32. Kirk and Raven, *The Presocratic Philosophers*, p. 2; E. R. Dodds, *Pagan and Christian in an Age of Anxiety*, "Plotinus" in the index; and Evelyn Underhill, *Mysticism*, "Plotinus" in the index (both in Bibliography under Mythology and Religion).

33. See Underhill, *Mysticism*, under appropriate index headings. Also see A. J. Arberry, *Sufism*, and Idries Shah, *The Sufis* (both in Bibliography under Mythology and Religion).

34. See Norman O. Brown, *Life Against Death*, ch. 10, "The Ambiguities of Sublimation"; and Marcuse, *Eros and Civilization*, "Sexuality" and "Sublimation" in the index (in Bibliography under The Lover, the Forms of Love, and Relationship).

35. The literature on individuation, or the process of becoming whole, as Jungians define the term, is enormous. But see, for an overview, Jacobi, *The Psychology of C. G. Jung*, "Wholeness" in the index. See also *The Portable Jung*, ch. 8, "Psychological Types," and ch. 9, "The Transcendent Function."

36. 1 John 4:8. See Eberhard Nestle et al., *Novum Testamentum Graece* (in Bibliography under Mythology and Religion).

37. See Anders Nygren, *Agape and Eros*, especially ch. 4 and p. 30 (in Bibliography under The Lover, the Forms of Love, and Relationship).

38. Ibid., p. 118.

39. See Moffatt's discussion of the meanings of agape in *Love in the New Testament*, pp. 44ff.

40. See Gene Outka's discussion in his *Agape: An Ethical Analysis*, p. 20 (in Bibliography under The Lover, the Forms of Love, and Relationship), and Nygren, *Agape and Eros*, p. 98.

41. This is certainly true if we adopt the Freudian understanding that libido as eros underlies all our human motivations, especially in the area of "love." Norman O. Brown pushes this Freudian idea to its logical conclusion. See Brown, *Life Against Death*.

42. Campbell, *The Masks of God*, "Amor" in the index.

43. Gal. 3:28.

44. This is to borrow Harville Hendrix's definition of intimate relationship in his *Getting the Love You Want*, p. 200 (in Bibliography under The Lover, the Forms of Love, and Relationship).

45. Martin Buber, *I and Thou* (in Bibliography under Theology and Philosophy).

46. See Marcuse, *Eros and Civilization*, "Pleasure principle" and "Reality principle" in the index.

CHAPTER 4: THE LOVER'S ORIGINS

1. See Robert Moore and Douglas Gillette, *King, Warrior, Magician, Lover: Rediscovering the Archetypes of Mature Masculinity*, pp. 33–37 (in Bibliography under Jungian Thought).

2. Ibid., pp. 15–27. See also Carl Jung, *Aion*, pp. 31 and 195 (in Bibliography under Jungian Thought).

3. For a thorough discussion of the nature of archetypes, see Jungian Thought in the Bibliography, and consult the indexes. Let us just note here that, in our view, archetypes are elaborations in human beings of more foundational instinctual configurations or "action patterns" inherited from our animal past. Archetypes are not Gods or Goddesses, as Jean Bolen tries to make them. They do not have personalities, nor do they exhibit personality types per se. Rather, they are truly transpersonal and subhuman. While, from our perspective, it

is often helpful for a man to "anthropomorphize" the four underlying
archetypes of the mature masculine—that is, to access them imaginally
by personalizing them—it is important to always keep in mind that
what we are really invoking is an *energy system*.

4. See Appendix B. Also, see Robin Fox's essay "Alliance and
Constraint: Sexual Selection in the Evolution of Human Kinship Sys-
tems" in Bernard Campbell, ed., *Sexual Selection and the Descent of
Man 1871–1971* (in Bibliography under Anthropology).

5. See, for example, Konrad Lorenz, *On Aggression*, especially
chs. 7 and 11 (in Bibliography under Anthropology).

6. In addition to studies by Jane Goodall and Frans de Waal (both
in Bibliography under Primate Ethology), see Edward O. Wilson's
discussion in *On Human Nature*, ch. 7 (in Bibliography under The
Lover, the Forms of Love, and Relationship).

7. John 15:13.

8. Joseph Campbell, *The Power of Myth*, p. 110 (in Bibliography
under Mythology and Religion).

9. The literature in this area is growing. See, for example, Anne
Moir and David Jessel, *Brain Sex: The Real Difference Between Men
and Women*, ch. 4 (in Bibliography under The Lover, the Forms of
Love, and Relationship); and Anthony Stevens, *Archetypes: A Natural
History of the Self*, especially chs. 10 and 11 (in Bibliography under
Jungian Thought).

10. The research on the genetic foundations of a wide range of
human behaviors, including characteristically male and female behaviors, is just now coming of age. For a succinct, though not thorough,
discussion of the evidence, see Moir and Jessel, *Brain Sex*, especially
chs. 1–3.

11. See Lillian Robin, *Intimate Strangers: Men and Women
Together*, especially ch. 3 (in Bibliography under The Lover, the
Forms of Love, and Relationship). Also see Stevens, *Archetype*, ch. 11.

12. See Jungian Thought in the Bibliography, and consult
"Anima" and "Animus" in the indexes.

13. The thought here is that contrast and complimentarity between the genders intensify the attraction of the sexes for each other.

14. See, for example, Mary Daley, *Beyond God the Father: To-
ward a Philosophy of Women's Liberation* or her *Gyn/Ecology* and
Rosemary Ruether's somewhat more moderate *Sexism and God-Talk:
Toward a Feminist Theology* (in Bibliography under Theology and

Philosophy), and Riane Eisler, *The Chalice and the Blade: Our History, Our Future* (in Bibliography under Anthropology). See also the shallow, snippy indictment of male scientists by Carol Tavris, *The Mismeasure of Woman* (in Bibliography under Anthropology).

15. See Anthony Storr, *Human Aggression*, especially ch. 7 (in Bibliography under Other Psychologies); also R. L. McNeely and Gloria Robinson-Simpson, "The Truth About Domestic Violence: A Falsely Framed Issue," in *Social Work* magazine (in Bibliography under Anthropology).

16. Sam Keen, *The Passionate Life*, chs. 4, 8, and 9 (in Bibliography under The Lover, the Forms of Love, and Relationship).

CHAPTER 5: HIS PATH THROUGH THE GARDEN

1. The God associated with the creative divine Word was Ptah. See Henri Frankfort, *Ancient Egyptian Religion*, pp. 23–24 (in Bibliography under Mythology and Religion).

2. Gen. 1:3.

3. Stephen Mitchell, ed. and trans. *The Selected Poetry of Rainer Maria Rilke*, p. 151 (in Bibliography under Literature).

4. See Swami Nikhilananda's discussion of Brahman in *The Upanishads*, Vol. 1, "Discussion of Brahman in the Upanishads" (in Bibliography under Theology and Philosophy).

5. A term often used in the new age movement to denote a more mystical, inclusive level of awareness. See, for example, Charles Fillmore, "Jesus Christ's Atonement," in Lowell Fillmore, ed., *Unity Treasure Chest*, p. 70 (in Bibliography under Theology and Philosophy).

6. Louis Untermeyer, ed., *A Treasury of Great Poems, English and American*, pp. 603, 600 (in Bibliography under Literature).

7. Walt Whitman, *Leaves of Grass* (in Bibliography under Literature).

8. From Wallace Stevens's poem "Peter Quince at the Clavier," in Wallace Stevens, *The Palm at the End of the Mind: Selected Poems and a Play*, pp. 8–10 (in Bibliography under Literature).

9. 'Abd-al-Rahmān 'Azzām, *The Eternal Message of Muhammad*, p. 30 (in Bibliography under Mythology and Religion).

10. From Alfred, Lord Tennyson, "Higher Pantheism," in Al-

fred, Lord Tennyson, *Idylls of the King*, p. 297 (in Bibliography under Literature).

11. J.R.R. Tolkien, *The Tolkien Reader*, p. 68 (in Bibliography under Literature).

12. This reference, used again and again throughout Christian poetry and other writings, is to the image in Genesis 3:24 of the fierce angelic figure with the flaming sword that God placed at the gate to the Garden of Eden to keep Adam and Eve, and their descendants, forever after from reentering Paradise.

13. The poet Robert Bly's phrase.

14. John 20:14–16. We say "rightly—for the gardener" because the Lover archetype expressed through the saving power of regenerated life has always been celebrated in mythology and poetry as the divine Gardner, the fertilizing and stewarding ecological force.

15. Joseph Campbell, *The Power of Myth*, pp. 34–35 (in Bibliography under Mythology and Religion). Recently, it has been speculated that the letter circulated in Chief Seattle's name is spurious.

16. Ibid., pp. 34–35.

17. See Edward Edinger, *Ego and Archetype*, "Ego-Self axis" in the index (in Bibliography under Jungian Thought).

18. Erich Neumann, *Art and the Creative Unconscious*, p. 167 (in Bibliography under The Lover, the Forms of Love, and Relationship).

19. As documented in a recent PBS special on the culture of Bali.

20. Mark 8:18.

21. See Carl Jung, *Man and His Symbols*, Pt. 4 (in Bibliography under Jungian Thought).

22. Ibid., p. 287.

23. Ibid., p. 292.

24. Ibid., p. 293.

25. Ibid., p. 306.

26. 1 Cor. 13:12.

27. Robert Graves, *The Greek Myths*, vol. 1, p. 56 (in Bibliography under Mythology and Religion).

28. Exod. 19:21.

29. Jung, *Man and His Symbols*, p. 309.

30. Ibid.

31. See Alan Watts, *The Supreme Identity: An Essay on Oriental Metaphysic and the Christian Religion*, pp. 84–91 (in Bibliography under Theology and Philosophy).

32. See Robert Moore and Douglas Gillette, *The Magician Within* (in Bibliography under Jungian Thought).

33. See S. H. Hooke, *Middle Eastern Mythology*, pp. 79–87 (in Bibliography under Mythology and Religion). Also see James B. Pritchard, *The Ancient Near East*, vol. 1, pp. 92ff (in Bibliography under Mythology and Religion).

34. The literature in this area is growing rapidly. As one of the best discussions of human reproductive strategies, see Donald Symons, *The Evolution of Human Sexuality* (in Bibliography under Anthropology). The idea is, essentially, that human males tend to be somewhat more inclined than females to seek multiple sexual partners. At the most primordial level, this reflects the differences between men and women both in terms of their capacities to reproduce and in terms of their relative biological investments in particular offspring.

CHAPTER 6: THE LOVER IN HIS FULLNESS

1. Herbert Marcuse, *Eros and Civilization: A Philosophical Inquiry into Freud*, p. xv (in Bibliography under The Lover, the Forms of Love, and Relationship).

2. For a Jungian understanding of this term, see Erich Neumann, *Art and the Creative Unconscious*, "Participation Mystique," in the index (in Bibliography under The Lover, the Forms of Love, and Relationship).

3. Marcuse, *Eros and Civilization*, p. 11.

4. Ibid., p. 12.

5. Ibid.

6. Ibid., p. 14.

7. Ibid., p. 19.

8. Ibid., p. 141.

9. Ibid., p. 25.

10. Ibid., p. 29.

11. Ibid., p. 11.

12. See Paul Tillich's discussion in his *Systematic Theology: III*, pp. 406ff (in Bibliography under Theology and Philosophy).

13. Norman Brown's term.

14. Matt. 10:8. See Paul Tillich's sermon on this theme in his *The Eternal Now*, ch. 5 (in Bibliography under Theology and Philosophy).

CHAPTER 7: THE IMPOTENT: LOST IN THE WASTELAND

1. As Theodore Millon demonstrates in his *Disorders of Personality: DSM III: Axis II* manual (in Bibliography under Other Psychologies).

2. The literature in this field is growing rapidly, both in terms of anthropological investigation and in terms of popular interpretations. For a representative sampling, see Robert Bly, *Iron John: A Book About Men* (in Bibliography under Literature); Mircea Eliade, *Rites and Symbols of Initiation: The Mysteries of Birth and Rebirth* (in Bibliography under Mythology and Religion); David Gilmore, *Manhood in the Making: Cultural Concepts of Masculinity* (in Bibliography under Anthropology); Joseph Henderson, *Thresholds of Initiation* (in Bibliography under Mythology and Religion); Gilbert Herdt, *Rituals of Manhood: Male Initiation in Papua New Guinea* (in Bibliography under Anthropology); Robert Moore and Douglas Gillette, *King, Warrior, Magician, Lover: Rediscovering the Archetypes of the Mature Masculine; The King Within: Accessing the King in the Male Psyche; The Warrior Within: Accessing the Knight in the Male Psyche;* and *The Magician Within: Accessing the Shaman in the Male Psyche* (all in Bibliography under Jungian Thought); and Hutton Webster, *Primitive Secret Societies* (in Bibliography under Anthropology).

3. Ethological evidence indicates that females can tolerate a greater element of fear in their relationships and still remain sexually interested than can males. In males, aggression and sexuality are often linked, whereas it seems likely that males have selected females to mate with who have demonstrated greater overall tendencies toward relative submissiveness. See Bernard Campbell, ed., *Sexual Selection and the Descent of Man 1871–1971*, especially chs. 9 and 10 (in Bibliography under Anthropology); Herant A. Katchadourian, ed., *Human Sexuality: A Comparative and Developmental Perspective* (in Bibliography under The Lover, the Forms of Love, and Relationship); Konrad Lorenz, *On Aggression,* especially chs. 3, 4, and 7 (in Bibliography under Anthropology); Eugene Monick, *Phallos: Sacred Image of the Masculine,* chs. 1, 3, and 7 (in Bibliography under The Lover, the Forms of Love, and Relationship); Anthony Storr, *Human Aggression,* ch. 7, especially pp. 67–70, 72, 74–75; and Donald Symons, *The*

Evolution of Human Sexuality, "Sex Differences," "Sexual Arousal," "Sexual Attractiveness," and "Sexual Selection" in the index (in Bibliography under Anthropology).

4. Often, women have difficulty understanding the extremely sensitive nature of phallus and erection. They cannot understand why men cannot will their penises to become engorged, nor do they comprehend the various disempowering factors in a man's environment that militate against erection. In terms of the environment of the relationship itself, women seldom realize the guilt and shame-inducing emotional power they have over men, largely due to male sensitivity to "mother issues." Most men cannot "get it up" if they feel significantly disempowered or if they feel regressed into the mother-son mode of relating. See Monick, *Phallos: Sacred Image of the Masculine*, pp. 22–25, 43–56.

CHAPTER 8: THE ADDICT:
POSSESSION BY THE LOVER WITHIN

1. Theodore Millon, *Disorders of Personality: DSM-III: Axis II*, ch. 5 (in Bibliography under Other Psychologies).

2. Ibid., ch. 7.

3. Ibid., p. 337.

4. Ibid., pp. 61, 92, 244–272.

5. See Robert Moore and Douglas Gillette, *The Warrior Within: Accessing the Knight in the Male Psyche*, "Masochist" and "Sadist" in the index (in Bibliography under Jungian Thought).

6. See Reinhold Niebuhr, *The Nature and Destiny of Man*, vol. 2, *Human Nature*, "Sin" in the index (in Bibliography under Theology and Philosophy).

7. Jung combined his insight that many illnesses are symbolic of psychic distress in quite specific ways with his belief that the central ailment of modern people is their alienation from a spiritual dimension to help the founder of AA develop his ideas about the interrelationship between the Ego and the Higher Power as well as the technology of the twelve-step program.

8. See Robert Moore and Douglas Gillette, *The Magician Within: Accessing the Shaman in the Male Psyche*, "Shaman" in the index (in Bibliography under Jungian Thought).

CHAPTER 9: EMBODYING THE LOVER WITHIN

1. Herbert Marcuse, *Eros and Civilization*, pp. 84–85, 144, 184ff (in Bibliography under The Lover, the Forms of Love, and Relationship); Erich Neumann, *Art and the Creative Unconscious*, especially ch. 4 (in Bibliography under The Lover, the Forms of Love, and Relationships); and for an understanding of the self-satisfying power of artistic endeavor as a part of our primate heritage, see Desmond Morris and Ramona Morris, *Men and Apes*, pp. 250–254 (in Bibliography under Primate Ethology).

2. Carl Jung, "Marriage as a Psychological Relationship," in *The Portable Jung*, ed. Joseph Campbell, pp. 163–177 (in Bibliography under Jungian Thought).

3. Based on Denis de Rougemont's classic, *Love in the Western World* (in Bibliography under The Lover, the Forms of Love, and Relationship).

EPILOGUE: JOY TO THE WORLD: RETURNING TO THE GARDEN THROUGH LOVE

1. Matt. 25:31–46.
2. Luke 17:21.
3. For example, Matt. 24:3–44; and Acts 2:19.
4. Isa. 11:6–8, 65:25.
5. Paraphrase of verse 77 from "The Gospel of Thomas," in *The Nag Hammadi Library*, Ed. James M. Robinson, p. 126 (in Bibliography under Mythology and Religion).

APPENDIX B: ARCHETYPES AND THE LIMBIC SYSTEM

The argument of this appendix owes a great debt to George S. Everly, Jr.'s synthesis of the most recent work of a number of brain researchers in his paper "The Biological Bases of Personality: The Contribution of Paleocortical Anatomy and Physiology to Personality and Personality Disorders." He presented this paper at the First International Congress on Disorders of Personality in Copenhagen, Denmark, in August 1988.

1. Paul D. MacLean, *The Triune Brain in Evolution: Role in Paleocerebral Functions*, p. 257 (in Bibliography under Brain Research).

2. Ibid., p. 264.

3. Ibid., in toto.

4. Everly, "Biological Bases of Personality," p. 5.

5. Ibid., p. 5.

6. Ibid., p. 5.

7. Ibid., p. 5.

8. Ibid., p. 6.

9. MacLean, *Triune Brain in Evolution*, ch. 21.

10. Everly, "Biological Bases of Personality," p. 7.

11. Everly, "Biological Bases of Personality," p. 8; and MacLean, *Triune Brain in Evolution*, ch. 19.

12. MacLean, *Triune Brain in Evolution*, pp. 322ff.

13. Everly, "Biological Bases of Personality," p. 9; and MacLean, *Triune Brain in Evolution*, chs. 18–27.

14. MacLean, *Triune Brain in Evolution*, pp. 497, 498, ch. 27.

APPENDIX C: ARCHETYPES AND THE ANIMA

1. See Alice Miller's discussion of "poisonous pedagogy" and the role of the mother in destroying her children's sense of Self (in Bibliography under Other Psychologies).

2. An example of this can be found in the Canaanite Ba'al cycle of myths. In them Ba'al, king of the created world, has two enemies to defeat—chaos (Yamm) and death (Mot). He succeeds against Yamm, but is slain by Mot. His sister and his queen, Anath, kills Mot and resurrects Ba'al. Anath further proves herself to be Ba'al's comrade-in-arms when she summons his enemies to a banquet, locks the doors, and kills them all.

BIBLIOGRAPHY

1. *ANTHROPOLOGY*

Ardrey, Robert. *African Genesis: A Personal Investigation into the Animal Origins and Nature of Man.* New York: Dell, 1963.
————. *The Social Contract: A Personal Inquiry into the Evolutionary Sources of Order and Disorder.* New York: Dell, 1971.
Campbell, Bernard, ed. *Sexual Selection and the Descent of Man, 1871–1971.* Chicago: Aldine, 1972.
Clemente, C. D., and Donald B. Lindsley, eds. *Aggression and Defense: Neural Mechanisms and Social Patterns.* Vol. 5. Berkeley: University of California Press, 1967.
Corballis, Michael C. *The Lopsided Ape: Evolution of the Generative Mind.* New York: Oxford University Press, 1991.

Dart, Raymond A. "The Predatory Transition from Ape to Man." *International Anthropological and Linguistic Review* 1 (1953): 201–219.

Diamond, Jared. *The Third Chimpanzee: The Evolution and Future of the Human Animal.* New York: HarperCollins, 1992.

Eisler, Riane. *The Chalice and the Blade: Our History, Our Future.* San Francisco: Harper & Row, 1988.

Feilds, Rick. *The Code of the Warrior in History, Myth, and Everyday Life.* New York: HarperCollins, 1991.

Gillette, Douglas. Review of David Gilmore, *Manhood in the Making.* In *Wingspan: A Journal of the Male Spirit* (Spring 1991):12.

Gilmore, David. *Manhood in the Making: Cultural Concepts of Masculinity.* New Haven: Yale University Press, 1990.

Herdt, Gilbert H., ed. *Rituals of Manhood: Male Initiation in Papua New Guinea.* Berkeley: University of California Press, 1982.

Johnson, Roger N. *Aggression in Man and Animals.* Philadelphia: W. B. Saunders, 1972.

Klein, Richard G. *The Human Career: Human Biological and Cultural Origins.* Chicago: University of Chicago Press, 1989.

Laughlin, William S. "Hunting: An Integrating Biobehavior System and Its Evolutionary Importance." In *Man the Hunter,* edited by Richard B. Lee and Irven DeVore. Chicago: Aldine, 1968.

Leakey, Louis S. B. "Development of Aggression as a Factor in Early Human and Pre-Human Evolution." In *Aggression and Defense,* edited by C. D. Clemente and D. B. Lindsley. Berkeley: University of California Press, 1967.

Life Editors. *The Epic of Man.* New York: Time, 1961.

Lopez, Barry Holstrum. *Of Wolves and Men.* New York: Charles Scribner's Sons, 1978.

Lorenz, Konrad. *On Aggression.* San Diego: Harcourt Brace Jovanovich, 1966; Munich: Deutscher Taschenbuch, 1963

MacKinnon, Michael. *The Ape Within Us.* New York: Holt, Rinehart and Winston, 1978.

McNeely, R. L., and Gloria Robinson-Simpson. "The Truth About Domestic Violence." *Social Work,* November-December 1987, National Association of Social Workers.

Mahdi, Louise Carus, Steven Foster, and Meredith Little, eds. *Betwixt and Between: Patterns of Masculine and Feminine Initiation.* LaSalle, Ill.: Open Court, 1987.

Martin, Phyllis M., and Patrick O'Meara, eds. *Africa*. Bloomington: Indiana University Press, 1977.

Montagu, Ashley, ed. *Man and Aggression*. 2d ed. New York: Oxford University Press, 1973.

Rappaport, Roy A. "The Sacred in Human Evolution." *Annual Review of Ecology and Systematics* 2 (1971): 23–44.

Roper, M. K. "A Survey of the Evidence for Intrahuman Killing in the Pleistocene." *Current Anthropology* 10 (1989): 427–459.

Ruspoli, Mario. *The Cave of Lascaux: The Final Photographs*. New York: Harry N. Abrams, 1987.

Sagan, Carl, and Ann Druyan. *Shadows of Forgotten Ancestors: A Search for Who We Are*. New York: Random House, 1992.

Scott, John Paul. "Biological Basis of Human Warfare: An Interdisciplinary Problem." In *Interdisciplinary Relationships in the Social Sciences*, edited by Muzafer Sherif and Carolyn W. Sherif. Chicago: Aldine, 1969.

Smithsonian Editors. *Man and Beast: Comparative Social Behavior*. Edited by J. F. Eisenberg and Witton S. Dillon. Smithsonian Annual III. Washington, D.C.: Smithsonian Institution Press, 1971.

Symons, Donald. *The Evolution of Human Sexuality*. Oxford: Oxford University Press, 1979.

Tavris, Carol. *The Mismeasure of Woman: Why Women Are Not the Better Sex, the Inferior Sex, or the Opposite Sex*. New York: Simon & Schuster, 1992.

Tierney, Patrick. *The Highest Altar: Unveiling the Mystery of Human Sacrifice*. New York: Penguin Books, 1989.

Turner, Victor. *The Ritual Process: Structure and Anti-Structure*. Ithaca: Cornell University Press, 1969.

Webster, Hutton. *Primitive Secret Societies*. New York: Macmillan, 1932.

Wilson, Edward O. *Sociobiology: The Abridged Edition*. Cambridge: Harvard University Press, 1980.

———. *Sociobiology: The New Synthesis*. Cambridge: Harvard University Press, 1975.

Zillmann, Dolf. *Hostility and Aggression*. Hillsdale, N.J.: L. Erlbaum Associates, 1979.

2. *BRAIN RESEARCH*

Ashbrook, James B. *The Human Mind and the Mind of God: Theological Promise in Brain Research*. Lanham, Md.: University Press of America, 1984.

Harth, Erich. *Windows on the Mind: Reflections on the Physical Basis of Consciousness*. New York: Quill, 1983.

Jaynes, Julian. *The Origin of Consciousness in the Breakdown of the Bicameral Mind*. Boston: Houghton Mifflin, 1976.

MacLean, Paul D. *The Triune Brain in Evolution: Role in Paleocerebral Functions*. New York: Plenum Press, 1990.

Restak, Richard M. *The Brain*. New York: Bantam Books, 1984.

3. *HISTORY*

Albright, William F. *The Archeology of Palestine*. Harmondsworth, Middlesex, Eng.: Penguin Books, 1949.

Aldred, Cyril. *Akhenaten, Pharaoh of Egypt: A New Study*. 1968. Reprint. London: Sphere Books, Abacus, 1972.

"Andean Civilization." *Encyclopedia Britannica*. Vol. 1. Chicago: Encyclopedia Britannica, 1967, pp. 889–891.

Barnett, R. D., and Werner Forman. *Assyrian Palace Reliefs and Their Influence on the Sculptures of Babylon and Persia*. London: Batchworth Press.

Barr, Stringfellow. *The Will of Zeus: A History of Greece*. New York: Dell, 1965.

Berger, Peter L. *Facing up to Modernity: Excursions in Society, Politics, and Religion*. New York: Basic Books, 1977.

Blacker, Irwin R., and *Horizon* Magazine Editors. *Cortes and the Aztec Conquest*. New York: American Heritage, 1965.

Browning, Robert. *The Emperor Julian*. Berkeley: University of California Press, 1976.

Casson, Lionel et al. *Mysteries of the Past*. New York: American Heritage, 1977.

Cristofani, Mauro. *The Etruscans: A New Investigation*. Translated from Italian by Brian Phillips. New York: Orbis Books, 1979.

Edwards, I.E.S. *The Pyramids of Egypt.* Harmondsworth, Middlesex, Eng.: Penguin Books, 1947.

Gernet, Jacques. *A History of Chinese Civilization.* New York: Cambridge University Press, 1982. Originally published in French as *Le Monde chinois.* Paris: Librairie Armand Colin, 1972.

Gimbutas, Marija. *The Goddesses and Gods of Old Europe: Myths and Cult Images.* Berkeley: University of California Press, 1982.

Gurney, O. R. *The Hittites.* Harmondsworth, Middlesex, Eng.: Penguin Books, 1952.

Morley, Sylvanus G., and George W. Brainerd. *The Ancient Maya.* 4th ed. Revised by Robert J. Sharer. Stanford: Stanford University Press, 1983.

National Geographic Editors. *The Age of Chivalry.* Washington, D.C.: National Geographic Society, 1969.

Peterson, Frederick. *Ancient Mexico: An Introduction to the Pre-Hispanic Cultures.* 1959. Reprint. Toms River, N.J.: Capricorn Books, 1962.

Säve-Söderbergh, Torgny. *Pharaohs and Mortals.* New York: Bobbs-Merrill, 1961.

Steindorff, George, and Keith C. Seele. *When Egypt Ruled the East.* Chicago: University of Chicago Press, 1942.

Thompson, John Eric S. *The Rise and Fall of Maya Civilization.* Norman: University of Oklahoma Press, 1954. Especially Chapter 2.

Time Editors. *The Epic of Man.* New York: Time, 1961. Especially Chapter 7.

Time-Life Books Editors. *The Age of the God-Kings, 3000–1500 B.C..* New York: Time-Life Books, 1990.

Turnbull, Stephen R. *The Book of the Samurai: The Warrior Class of Japan.* New York: W. H. Smith Publishers, 1982.

Wilson, John A. *The Culture of Ancient Egypt.* Chicago: University of Chicago Press, 1951. Originally published as *The Burden of Egypt.*

4. JUNGIAN THOUGHT

Andrews, Valerie, Robert Bosnak, and Karen Walter Goodwin, eds. *Facing Apocalypse.* Dallas: Spring Publications, 1987.

Bolen, Jean Shinoda. *Goddesses in Every Woman: A New Psychology of Women*. New York: Harper & Row, 1984.

———. *Gods in Everyman: A New Psychology of Men's Lives and Loves*. San Francisco: Harper & Row, 1989.

Corneau, Guy. *Absent Fathers, Lost Sons: The Search for Masculine Identity*. Boston: Shambhala, 1991.

de Castillejo, Irene Claremont Day. *Knowing Woman: A Feminine Psychology*. New York: G. P. Putnam's Sons, 1973; New York: Harper & Row, 1974.

De Vries, Ad. *Dictionary of Symbols and Imagery*. Amsterdam: North-Holland Publishing Co., 1984.

Edinger, Edward F. *The Creation of Consciousness: Jung's Myth for Modern Man*. Toronto: Inner City Books, 1984.

———. *Ego and Archetype: Individuation and the Religious Function of the Psyche*. New York: G. P. Putnam's Sons, 1972; New York: Penguin Books, 1974.

Evans, Richard I. *Jung on Elementary Psychology: A Discussion Between C. G. Jung and Richard I. Evans*. New York: E. P. Dutton, 1976.

Garrison, Jim. *The Darkness of God: Theology After Hiroshima*. Grand Rapids, Mich.: William B. Eerdmans, 1982.

Hannah, Barbara. *Encounters with the Soul: Active Imagination as Developed by C. G. Jung*. Boston: Sigo Press, 1981.

———. *Jung: His Life and Work*. Boston: Shambhala, 1991.

Hillman, James et al. *Puer Papers*. Dallas: Spring Publications, 1979. Especially the chapter by James Hillman, "Senex and Puer: An Aspect of the Historical and Psychological Present."

Jacobi, Jolande. *Complex Archetype Symbol in the Psychology of C. G. Jung*. Princeton: Princeton University Press, 1959. Originally published in German as *Komplex/Archetypus/Symbol in der Psychologie C. G. Jung*. Zurich and Stuttgart: Rascher Verlag, 1957.

———. *The Psychology of C. G. Jung*. 1942. Reprint. New Haven: Yale University Press, 1973.

Jaffé, Aniela. *The Myth of Meaning: Jung and the Expansion of Consciousness*. New York: Penguin Books, 1975.

Jung, Carl G. *Aion: Researches into the Phenomenology of the Self*. Vol. 9 of *The Collected Works of C. G. Jung*. Princeton: Princeton University Press, 1959.

————. *Civilization in Transition.* Vol. 10 of *The Collected Works of C. G. Jung.* Princeton: Princeton University Press, 1970.

————. *Man and His Symbols.* New York: Dell, 1964; London: Aldus Books, 1964.

————. *Modern Man in Search of a Soul.* New York: Harcourt, Brace, 1933.

————. *Mysterium Coniunctionis: An Inquiry into the Separation and Synthesis of Psychic Opposites in Alchemy.* 2d ed. Princeton: Princeton University Press, 1970.

————. *The Portable Jung.* Edited by Joseph Campbell. New York: Penguin Books, 1971. Reprint of Jung's work in *Aion,* pp. 148ff.

————. *Psyche and Symbol: A Selection from the Writings of C. G. Jung.* Edited by Violet deLaszlo. Garden City, N.Y.: Doubleday, 1958.

————. *Psychology and Alchemy.* 2d ed. 1953. Reprint. Princeton: Princeton University Press, 1980.

————. *Psychology and Religion: West and East.* 2d ed. Vol. 11 of *The Collected Works of C. G. Jung.* Princeton: Princeton University Press, 1958.

Layard, John. *A Celtic Quest: Sexuality and Soul in Individuation.* Dallas: Spring Publications, 1975.

Moore, Robert, ed. *Carl Jung and Christian Spirituality.* Mahwah, N.J.: Paulist Press, 1988.

————. *The Magician and the Analyst: Ritual, Sacred Space, and Psychotherapy.* Chicago: Center for the Scientific Study of Religion, 1992.

Moore, Robert, and Douglas Gillette. *King, Warrior, Magician, Lover: Rediscovering the Archetypes of Mature Masculinity.* San Francisco: HarperCollins, 1990.

————. *The King Within: Accessing the King in the Male Psyche.* New York: William Morrow, 1991.

————. *The Warrior Within: Accessing the Knight in the Male Psyche.* New York: William Morrow, 1992.

————. *The Magician Within: Accessing the Shaman in the Male Psyche.* New York: William Morrow, 1993.

Moore, Robert, and Daniel Meckel, eds. *Jung and Christianity in Dialogue: Faith, Feminism, and Hermeneutics.* Mahwah, N.J.: Paulist Press, 1991.

Perry, John Weir. *Roots of Renewal in Myth and Madness: The*

Meaning of Psychotic Episodes. San Francisco: Jossey-Bass, 1976.

Sanford, John A. *Dreams: God's Forgotten Language*. New York: J. B. Lippincott, 1968.

———. *Evil: The Shadow Side of Reality*. New York: Crossroad, 1981.

Stein, Murray, ed. *Jungian Analysis*. Boston: Shambhala, 1984.

Stevens, Anthony. *Archetypes: A Natural History of the Self*. New York: Quill, 1983. Originally published as *Archetype: A Natural History of the Self*. London: Routledge & Kegan, 1982.

———. *The Roots of War: A Jungian Perspective*. New York: Paragon House, 1989.

Von Franz, Marie Louise. *Projection and Re-Collection in Jungian Psychology*. LaSalle, Ill.: Open Court, 1980. Originally published in German as *Spiegelungen der Seele: Projektion und innere Sammlung*. Stuttgart: Kreuz Verlag, 1978.

———. *Shadow and Evil in Fairy Tales*. Dallas: Spring Publications, 1974.

Wolff, Toni. "Structural Forms of the Feminine Psyche." Privately printed for the Students Association, C. G. Jung Institute, Zurich, July 1956.

5. *KINGSHIP*

Basham, Arthur L. *The Wonder That Was India: A Survey of the Culture of the Indian Sub-Continent Before the Coming of the Muslims*. 1954. Reprint. New York: Grove Press, 1959.

Bricker, Victoria Reifler. *The Indian Christ, the Indian King: The Historical Substrate of Maya Myth and Ritual*. Austin: University of Texas Press, 1981.

Chaney, William A. *The Cult of Kingship in Anglo-Saxon England: The Transition from Paganism to Christianity*. Berkeley: University of California Press, 1970.

Emery, Walter B. *Archaic Egypt*. Harmondsworth, Middlesex, Eng.: Penguin Books, 1961.

Engnell, Ivan. *Studies in Divine Kingship in the Ancient Near East*. 2d ed. Oxford: Basil Blackwell, 1967.

Evans-Pritchard, Edward E. *The Divine Kingship of the Shilluk of the Nilotic Sudan.* Cambridge, Eng.: Cambridge University Press, 1948.

Frankfort, Henri. *The Birth of Civilization in the Near East.* Garden City, N.Y.: Doubleday, 1956; Bloomington: Indiana University Press, 1959.

————. *Kingship and the Gods: A Study of Ancient Near Eastern Religion as the Integration of Society and Nature.* Chicago: University of Chicago Press, 1948.

Gadd, Cyril J. *Ideas of Divine Rule in the Ancient East.* Schweich Lectures on Biblical Archeology. London: British Academy, 1948.

Gonda, Jan. "Ancient Indian Kingship from the Religious Point of View." *Numen* 3 (1955): 36–71, 122–155; *Numen* 4 (1956): 4, 24–58, 127–164.

Grottanelli, Christiano. "Kingship in the Ancient Mediterranean World." *Encyclopedia of Religion* 8 (1987): 317–322.

Hadfield, Percival. *Traits of Divine Kingship in Africa.* Westport, Conn.: Greenwood Press, 1979.

Hocart, Arthur Maurice. *Kingship.* London: Oxford University Press, 1927.

Hooke, Samuel H. *Myth, Ritual, and Kingship: Essays on the Theory and Practice of Kingship in the Ancient Near East and in Israel.* 2d ed. Oxford: Clarendon Press, 1967.

Johnson, Aubrey R. *Sacral Kingship in Ancient Israel.* Cardiff: University of Wales Press, 1955.

Kantorowicz, Ernest H. *The King's Two Bodies: A Study in Mediaeval Political Theology.* Princeton: Princeton University Press, 1957.

Keightley, David N. "The Religious Commitment: Shang Theology and the Genesis of Chinese Political Culture." *History of Religions* 17, no. 2 (November 1977/February-May 1978): 211–225.

Kenik, Helen A. "Code of Conduct for a King: Psalm 101." *Journal of Biblical Literature* 95, no. 3 (1976): 391–403.

Kwanten, Luc. *Imperial Nomads: A History of Central Asia, 500–1500.* Philadelphia: University of Pennsylvania Press, 1979.

Malandra, William W. *An Introduction to Ancient Iranian Religion: Readings from the "Avesta" and "Achaemenid" Inscriptions.* Minneapolis: University of Minnesota Press, 1983.

Meyerowitz, Eva L. R. *The Divine Kingship in Ghana and Ancient Egypt.* London: Faber & Faber, 1940.

Moore, Robert, and Douglas Gillette. *The King Within: Accessing the King in the Male Psyche*. New York: William Morrow, 1992.

Mumford, Lewis. *The City in History: Its Origins, Transformations, and Prospects*. New York: Harcourt, Brace and World, 1968.

Murray, Margaret Alice. "Evidence for the Custom of Killing the King in Ancient Egypt." *Man* 14 (1914): 17–23. London: Royal Anthropological Institute, 1914.

Myers, Henry Allen. *Medieval Kingship*. Chicago: Nelson-Hall, 1982.

Parrinder, Edward G. "Divine Kingship in West Africa." *Numen* 3 (1956): 111–121.

Peters, Edward. *The Shadow King: Rex Inutilis in Medieval Law and Literature, 751–1327*. New Haven: Yale University Press, 1970.

Richards, J. W. "Sacral Kings of Iran." *Mankind Quarterly* 20, nos. 1–2 (1979): 143–160.

Ruttan, Karl. "The Evolution of the Kingship Archetype in the Old Testament." Thesis, Chicago Theological Seminary, 1975.

Schele, Linda, and David A. Freidel. *A Forest of Kings: The Untold Story of the Ancient Maya*. New York: William Morrow, 1990.

Seligman, C. G. *Egypt and Negro Africa: A Study in Divine Kingship*. London: G. Routledge and Sons, 1934.

Tucci, Giuseppe. "The Secret Characters of the Kings of Ancient Tibet." *East and West* 6, no. 3 (October 1955): 197–205.

Valeri, Valerio. *Kingship and Sacrifice: Ritual and Society in Ancient Hawaii*. Translated from Hawaiian by Paula Wissing. Chicago: University of Chicago Press, 1985.

Waida, Manabu. "Notes on Sacred Kingship in Central Asia." *Numen* 23 (December 1976): 179–190.

———. "Sacred Kingship in Early Japan." Ph.D. diss., University of Chicago, 1974.

———. "Sacred Kingship in Early Japan: A Historical Introduction." *History of Religions* 15, no. 4 (May 1976): 319–342.

———. "Symbolism of 'Descent' in Tibetan Sacred Kingship and Some East Asian Parallels." *Numen* 20 (April 1973): 60–78.

Wales, Horace G. *The Mountain of God: A Study in Early Religion and Kingship*. London: Bernard Quaritch, 1953.

Zuidema, R. Tom. "The Lion in the City: Royal Symbols of Transition in Cuzco." *Journal of Latin American Lore* 9, no. 1 (Summer 1983): 39–100.

6. *LITERATURE*

Aeschylus. *Agamemnon*. In *Greek Literature in Translation*, edited by Whitney J. Oates and Charles T. Murphey. New York: David McKay, 1944.

Blake, William. *The Complete Poetry and Prose*. Rev. ed. Edited by David Erdman. Berkeley: University of California Press, 1981.

Bly, Robert. *Iron John: A Book About Men*. New York: Vintage, 1992.

Euripides. *The Bachae*. In *Euripides V*, edited by David Grene and Richmond Lattimore. New York: Washington Square Press, 1968.

Forster, E. M. *Passage to India*. New York: Harcourt, Brace and World, 1924.

Gibran, Kahlil. *The Prophet*. New York: Alfred A. Knopf, 1923.

Herbert, Frank. *Dune*. 1965. Reprint. New York: Putnam, 1984.

Hesse, Hermann. *Journey to the East*. Translated by Hilda Rosner. New York: Farrar, Straus & Giroux, 1956.

Jennings, Gary. *Aztec*. New York: Avon, 1980.

Lacy, Norris J., ed. *The Arthurian Encyclopedia*. New York: Garland, 1986.

Lewis, C. S. *The Four Loves*. New York: Harcourt Brace, 1960.

———. *'Til We Have Faces*. New York: Harcourt, Brace and World, 1956.

Mailer, Norman. *Ancient Evenings*. New York: Warner, 1983.

Márquez, Gabriel García. *Love in the Time of Cholera*. New York: Penguin Books, 1989.

Okri, Ben. *The Famished Road*. New York: Nan A. Talese/Doubleday, 1991.

Rilke, Rainer Maria. *The Selected Poetry*. Edited and translated by Stephen Mitchell. New York: Vintage, 1989 (reprint).

The Rubáiyát of Omar Khayyám. Edited by Manoocher Aryanpur. Kansas City: Hallmark Cards, 1967.

Sophocles. *Sophocles I*. Edited by David Grene and Richmond Lattimore. Chicago: University of Chicago Press, 1954.

Stevens, Wallace. *The Palm at the End of the Mind: Selected Poems and a Play*. New York: Random House, 1972.

Tennyson, Alfred. *Idylls of the King.* Edited by J. M. Gray. New Haven: Yale University Press, 1983.

Tolkien, J.R.R. *The Return of the King.* New York: Ballantine, 1965.

———. *The Tolkien Reader.* New York: Ballantine, 1966.

Untermeyer, Louis, ed. *A Treasury of Great Poems, English and American.* New York: Simon & Schuster, 1942.

White, T. H. *The Book of Merlyn.* Austin: University of Texas Press, 1977.

———. *The Once and Future King.* London: Collins, 1958; New York: Putnam, 1958.

Whitman, Walt. *Leaves of Grass.* New York: Random House, 1977.

7. THE LOVER, THE FORMS OF LOVE, AND RELATIONSHIP

Baber, Asa. *Naked at the Gender Gap: A Man's View of the War Between the Sexes.* New York: Carol Publishing Group, 1992.

Bowlby, John. *Separation: Anxiety and Anger.* New York: Basic Books, 1973.

Brown, Norman O. *Life Against Death: The Psychoanalytic Meaning of History.* Middletown, Conn.: Wesleyan University Press, 1959.

Cogniat, Raymond. *Chagall.* New York: Crown Publishers.

De Rougemont, Denis. *Love in the Western World.* 1956. Reprint. New York: Harper Colophon Books, 1974.

Fisher, Helen E. *Anatomy of Love: The Natural History of Monogamy, Adultery, and Divorce.* New York: W. W. Norton, 1992.

———. *The Sex Contract: The Evolution of Human Behavior.* New York: Quill, 1983.

Gillette, Douglas. "Men and Intimacy." *Wingspan: A Journal of the Male Spirit,* September 1990, pp. 9–10.

Grimal, Pierre. *Love in Ancient Rome.* New York: Crown, 1967.

Hendrix, Harville. *Getting the Love You Want.* New York: Henry Holt, 1988.

———. *Keeping the Love You Find: A Guide for Singles.* New York: Pocket Books, 1992.

Johnson, Robert. *We: Understanding the Psychology of Romantic Love.* San Francisco: Harper & Row, 1983.

Katchadourian, Herant A., ed. *Human Sexuality: A Comparative and Developmental Perspective.* Berkeley: University of California Press, 1979.

Keen, Sam. *The Passionate Life: Stages of Loving.* San Francisco: Harper & Row, 1983.

Lewinsohn, Richard. *A History of Sexual Customs.* New York: Bell, 1956.

Marcuse, Herbert. *Eros and Civilization: A Philosophical Inquiry into Freud.* Boston: Beacon Press, 1955.

May, Rollo. *Love and Will.* New York: W. W. Norton, 1969.

Moffatt, James. *Love in the New Testament.* London: Hodder & Stoughton, 1929.

Moir, Anne, and David Jessel. *Brain Sex: The Real Difference Between Men and Women.* New York: Carol Publishing Group, 1991.

Monick, Eugene. *Phallos: Sacred Image of the Masculine.* Toronto: Inner City Books, 1987.

Morgan, Elaine. *The Descent of Woman.* New York: Stein and Day, 1972.

Morris, Desmond. *Intimate Behavior.* New York: Random House, 1971.

———. *The Naked Ape: A Zoologist's Study of the Human Animal.* New York: McGraw-Hill, 1967.

Mountfield, David. *Greek and Roman Erotica.* New York: Crescent Books, 1982.

Neumann, Erich. *Art and the Creative Unconscious.* Princeton: Princeton University Press, 1959.

Nygren, Anders. *Agape and Eros.* Translated from Swedish by Philip S. Watson. Philadelphia: Westminster Press, 1953.

O'Donovan, Oliver. *The Problem of Self-Love in St. Augustine.* New Haven: Yale University Press, 1980.

Outka, Gene. *Agape: An Ethical Analysis.* New Haven: Yale University Press, 1972.

Pedersen, Loren E. *Dark Hearts: The Unconscious Forces That Shape Men's Lives.* Boston: Shambhala, 1991.

Reich, Wilhelm. *Sex-Pol: Essays, 1929–1934.* New York: Vintage, 1972.

Reichel-Dolmatoff, Gerardo. *Amazonian Cosmos: The Sexual and Religious Symbolism of the Tukano Indians.* Translated from

Spanish by the author. Chicago: University of Chicago Press, 1971.

Reik, Theodor. *Of Love and Lust*. New York: Jason Aronson, 1949, 1974.

Robin, Lillian. *Intimate Strangers: Men and Women Together*. San Bernardino, CA: The Borgo Press, 1990.

Sanford, John A. *The Invisible Partners: How the Male and Female in Each of Us Affects Our Relationships*. New York: Paulist Press, 1980.

Spink, Walter M. *The Axis of Eros*. New York: Penguin Books, 1975.

Tannen, Deborah. *You Just Don't Understand: Women and Men in Conversation*. New York: William Morrow, 1990.

Wallace, Robert A. *The Genesis Factor*. New York: William Morrow, 1979.

Watts, Alan, and Eliot Elisofan. *Erotic Spirituality: The Vision of Konarak*. Photographs by Eliot Elisofan. Commentary by Alan Watts. New York: Macmillan/Collier Books, 1971.

Wilson, Edward O. *On Human Nature*. Cambridge: Harvard University Press, 1978.

8. *MYTHOLOGY AND RELIGION*

Albright, William F. *Yahweh and the Gods of Canaan: A Historical Analysis of Two Contrasting Faiths*. Garden City, N.Y.: Doubleday, 1968.

Anderson, William. *Green Man: The Archetype of Our Oneness with the Earth*. London: HarperCollins, 1990.

Arberry, A. J. *Sufism: An Account of the Mystics of Islam*. New York: Harper & Row/Harper Torchbooks, 1970.

'Azzam, 'Abd-al-Rahman. *The Eternal Message of Muhammad*. New York: New American Library, 1965.

Baba, Pagal. *Temple of the Phallic King: The Mind of India: Yogis, Swamis, Sufis, and Avatars*. New York: Simon & Schuster, 1973.

Barnstone, Willis, ed. *The Other Bible*. San Francisco: Harper & Row, 1984.

Breasted, James H. *The Dawn of Conscience: The Sources of Our Moral Heritage in the Ancient World*. New York: Charles Scribner's Sons, 1933.

Budge, E. A. Wallis. *The Egyptian Book of the Dead (The Papyrus of Ani): Egyptian Text, Transliteration, and Translation.* New York: Dover, 1976.

Campbell, Joseph. *The Hero with a Thousand Faces.* Rev. ed. Princeton: Princeton University Press, 1968.

―――. *Historical Atlas of World Mythology.* Vol. 2. *The Way of the Seeded Earth.* Part 1: *The Sacrifice.* New York: Harper & Row/Perennial Library, 1988.

―――. *The Masks of God: Creative Mythology.* New York: Penguin Books, 1970.

―――. *The Masks of God: Occidental Mythology.* New York: Viking, 1964; New York: Penguin Books, 1976.

―――. *The Mythic Image.* Princeton: Princeton University Press, 1974.

―――. *The Power of Myth.* Garden City, N.Y.: Doubleday, 1988.

Carrasco, David. *Quetzalcoatl and the Irony of Empire: Myths and Prophecies in the Aztec Tradition.* Chicago: University of Chicago Press, 1982.

Cohn-Haft, Louis. *Source Readings in Ancient History: The Ancient Near East.* New York: Thomas Y. Crowell, 1965.

Confucius. *The Analects of Confucius.* Translated by Arthur Waley. 1938. Reprint. New York: Random House/Vintage, 1989.

Cumont, Franz. *The Mysteries of Mithra.* 1903. Reprint. New York: Dover, 1956.

Dodds, E. R. *Pagan and Christian in an Age of Anxiety: Some Aspects of Religious Experience from Marcus Aurelius to Constantine.* New York: W. W. Norton, 1965.

Dupont-Sommer, André. *The Essene Writings from Qumran.* New York: World/Meridian Books, 1961.

Eliade, Mircea. *Cosmos and History: The Myth of the Eternal Return.* 1954. Reprint. New York: Harper & Row, 1959.

―――. *Myth and Reality.* New York: Harper & Row/Harper Torchbooks, 1963.

―――. *Patterns in Comparative Religion.* New York: World Publishing, 1963. Originally published in French as *Traité d'histoire des religions.*

―――. *Rites and Symbols of Initiation: The Mysteries of Birth and Rebirth.* New York: Harper & Row, 1958.

―――. *The Sacred and the Profane: The Nature of Religion: The*

Significance of Religious Myth, Symbolism, and Ritual Within Life and Culture. New York: Harcourt, Brace and World, 1959. Originally published in German. Reinbek: Rowohlt Taschenbuch Verlag, 1957.

Evans-Wentz, Walter Y., ed. *The Tibetan Book of the Great Liberation; or the Method of Realizing Nirvana Through Knowing the Mind.* London: Oxford University Press, 1954.

Forsyth, Neil. *The Old Enemy: Satan and the Combat Myth.* Princeton: Princeton University Press, 1987.

Frankfort, Henri. *Ancient Egyptian Religion.* 1948. Reprint. New York: Harper & Row, 1961.

Frazer, James G. *The Golden Bough: A Study in Magic and Religion,* 13 vols. 1st ed. 1890. Reprint. New York: St. Martin's, 1969.

Gaer, Joseph. *How the Great Religions Began.* 1929. New rev. ed. New York: New American Library/Signet Books, 1954.

Godwin, Joscelyn. *Mystery Religions in the Ancient World.* San Francisco: Harper & Row, 1981.

Grant, Robert M. *Gnosticism and Early Christianity.* New York: Columbia University Press, 1959; New York: Harper & Row/Harper Torchbooks, 1959.

Graves, Robert. *The Greek Myths.* 2 vols. Harmondsworth, Middlesex, Eng.: Penguin Books, 1955.

Hadas, Moses. *The Apocrypha: An American Translation.* New York: Alfred A. Knopf and Random House, 1959.

Hamilton, Edith. *Mythology: Timeless Tales of Gods and Heroes.* New York: New American Library, 1940.

Henderson, Joseph L. *Thresholds of Initiation.* Middleton, Conn.: Wesleyan University Press, 1967.

Hooke, Samuel H. *Middle Eastern Mythology.* New York: Penguin, 1963.

James, William. *The Varieties of Religious Experience: A Study in Human Nature.* 1902. Reprint with a foreword by Jacques Barzun. New York: New American Library, 1958.

Jobes, Gertrude. *Dictionary of Mythology, Folklore, and Symbols.* Metuchen, N.J.: Scarecrow Press, 1962.

Kipnis, Aaron R. *Knights Without Armor.* Los Angeles: Jeremy P. Tarcher, 1991.

The Koran. Translated by N. J. Dawood. Baltimore: Penguin Books, 1956.

Kramer, Samuel Noah. *Sumerian Mythology: A Study of Spiritual and Literary Achievement in the Third Millennium B.C.* New York: Harper & Row, 1961.

Krickenberg, Walter et al. *Pre-Columbian American Religions.* Translated from German by Stanley Davis. New York: Holt, Rinehart and Winston, 1968.

Lind, Millard C. *Yahweh Is a Warrior: The Theology of Warfare in Ancient Israel.* Scottdale, Pa.: Herald Press, 1980.

MacCana, Proinsias. *Celtic Mythology.* Rev. ed. London: Bedrick Books, 1985.

Malandra, William W. *An Introduction to Ancient Iranian Religion: Readings from the Avesta and the Achaemenid Inscriptions.* Minneapolis: University of Minnesota Press, 1983.

Mansoor, Menachem. *The Dead Sea Scrolls.* Leiden, Netherlands: E. J. Brill, 1964; Grand Rapids, Mich.: William B. Eerdmans, 1964.

Matthews, John, ed. *Choirs of the God: Revisioning Masculinity.* San Francisco: HarperCollins, 1991.

May, Herbert G., and Bruce M. Metzger. *The New Oxford Annotated Bible with the Apocrypha.* Revised Standard Version. New York: Oxford University Press, 1977.

Miller, Patrick D. *The Divine Warrior in Early Israel.* Cambridge: Harvard University Press, 1973.

Moody, Raymond A. *Life After Life: The Investigation of a Phenomenon—Survival of Bodily Death.* With an introduction by Elisabeth Kübler-Ross. Saint Simons Island, Ga.: Mockingbird Books, 1975; New York: Bantam Books, 1975.

Mylonas, George E. *Eleusis and the Eleusinian Mysteries.* Princeton: Princeton University Press, 1961.

Novum Testamentum Graece. Edited by Eberhard Nestle et al. Stuttgart: Deutsche Bibelstiftung, 1979.

Oikonomides, A. N. *Mithraic Art: A Search for Unpublished and Unidentified Monuments.* Chicago: Ares, 1975.

Otto, Rudolf. *The Idea of the Holy.* New York: Oxford University Press, 1923.

Pagels, Elaine. *The Gnostic Gospels.* New York: Random House, 1979.

Perowne, Stewart. *Roman Mythology.* London: Hamlyn, 1969.

Perry, John Weir. *Lord of the Four Quarters: Myths of the Royal Father.* 1966. Reprint. New York: Macmillan/Collier Books, 1970.

————. *Lord of the Four Quarters: The Mythology of Kingship.* Mahwah, N.J.: Paulist Press, 1991.

Pritchard, James B., ed. *The Ancient Near East: An Anthology of Texts and Pictures.* Princeton: Princeton University Press, 1958.

Robinson, James M., ed. *The Nag Hammadi Library.* San Francisco: Harper & Row, 1977.

Scholem, Gershom. *Major Trends in Jewish Mysticism.* New York: Schocken Books, 1946.

————. *Origins of the Kaballah.* Edited by R. J. Werblowsky. Translated by Allan Arkush. Princeton: Princeton University Press (for the Jewish Publication Society), 1987. Originally published as *Ursprung und Anfänge der Kabbala.* Berlin: Walter de Gruyter, 1962.

Secret of the Golden Flower: A Chinese Book of Life, The. Translated by Richard Wilhelm. New York: Harcourt Brace Jovanovich, 1962.

Seltman, Charles T. *The Twelve Olympians.* New York: Thomas Y. Crowell, 1960.

Shah, Idries. *The Sufis.* Garden City, N.Y.: Doubleday/Anchor Books, 1964.

Smith, Huston. *Forgotten Truth: The Primordial Tradition.* New York: Harper & Row/Harper Colophon Books, 1976.

————. *The Religions of Man.* New York: Harper & Row, 1965.

Smith, Morton. *Jesus the Magician.* San Francisco: Harper & Row, 1978.

Sullivan, Lawrence, ed. *Healing and Restoring: Health and Medicine in the World's Religious Traditions.* New York: Macmillan, 1988.

Thomas, D. Winton, ed. *Documents from Old Testament Times.* Translated with introduction and notes by members of the Society for Old Testament Study. New York: Harper & Row, 1961.

Thompson, Brian. *The Story of Prince Rama.* Harmondsworth, Middlesex, Eng.: Penguin Books, 1980.

Underhill, Evelyn. *Mysticism.* New York: E. P. Dutton, 1911.

Vermes, Geza. *The Dead Sea Scrolls in English.* Baltimore: Penguin Books, 1962.

Walker, J.B.R. *The Comprehensive Concordance to the Holy Scriptures.* 1929. Reprint. New York: Macmillan, 1948.

Weston, Jesse L. *From Ritual to Romance: An Account of the Holy*

Grail from Ancient Ritual to Christian Symbol. 1920. Reprint. Garden City, N.Y.: Doubleday, 1957.

Wheatley, Paul. *The Pivot of the Four Quarters: A Preliminary Inquiry into the Origins and Character of the Ancient Chinese City*. Chicago: Aldine, 1971.

Williams, John Alden, ed. *Islam*. New York: Washington Square Press, 1961.

9. *OTHER PSYCHOLOGIES*

Ansbacher, Heinz L., and Rowena R. Ansbacher. *The Individual Psychology of Alfred Adler*. New York: Harper & Row, 1964.

Beahrs, John O. *Unity and Multiplicity: Multilevel Consciousness of Self in Hypnosis, Psychiatric Disorder and Mental Health*. New York: Brunner/Mazel, 1981.

Bettelheim, Bruno. *Freud and Man's Soul*. New York: Alfred A. Knopf, 1983.

Bradshaw, John. *Homecoming: Reclaiming and Championing Your Inner Child*. New York: Bantam Books, 1990.

Browning, Don S. *Generative Man: Psychoanalytic Perspectives*. Philadelphia: Westminster Press, 1973; New York: Dell, 1975.

Csikszentmihalyi, Mihaly. *Flow: The Psychology of Optimal Experience*. New York: HarperCollins, 1991.

Freud, Sigmund. *Moses and Monotheism*. Translated by Katherine Jones. New York: Alfred A. Knopf, 1939.

———. *Totem and Taboo: Some Points of Agreement Between the Mental Lives of Savages and Neurotics*. Translated by James Strachey. New York: W. W. Norton, 1950.

Keen, Sam. *Fire in the Belly: On Being a Man*. New York: Bantam Books, 1991.

Lauzun, Gérard. *Sigmund Freud: The Man and His Theories*. Translated by Patrick Evans. Greenwich, Conn.: Fawcett, 1962.

Lee, Ronald R., and John Colby Martin. *Psychotherapy After Kohut: A Textbook of Self Psychology*. Hillsdale, N.J.: Analytic Press, 1991.

Miller, Alice. *The Drama of the Gifted Child: How Narcissistic Parents Form and Deform the Emotional Lives of Their Talented Children*. New York: Basic Books, 1981. Originally published in

German as *Das Drama des begabten Kindes*. Frankfurt am Main: Suhrkamp, 1979.

————. *For Your Own Good: Hidden Cruelty in Child-Rearing and the Roots of Violence*. New York: Farrar Straus & Giroux, 1984. Originally published in German as *Am Anfang war Erziehung*. Frankfurt am Main: Suhrkamp, 1980.

————. *Thou Shalt Not Be Aware: Society's Betrayal of the Child*. New York: Farrar Straus & Giroux, 1984. Originally published in German as *Du sollst nicht merken*. Frankfurt am Main: Suhrkamp, 1981.

Millon, Theodore. *Disorders of Personality: DSM-III: Axis II*. New York: John Wiley & Sons, 1981.

————. *Modern Psychopathology: A Biosocial Approach to Maladaptive Learning and Functioning*. Prospect Heights, Ill.: Waveland Press, 1983.

Peck, M. Scott. *People of the Lie: The Hope for Healing Human Evil*. New York: Simon & Schuster, 1983. ·

————. *The Road Less Traveled: A New Psychology of Love, Traditional Values and Spiritual Growth*. New York: Simon & Schuster, 1978.

Rizzuto, Ana-Maria. *The Birth of the Living God: A Psychoanalytic Study*. Chicago: University of Chicago Press, 1979.

Rogers, David J. *Fighting to Win: Samurai Techniques for Your Work and Life*. Garden City, N.Y.: Doubleday, 1984.

Schmookler, Andrew Bard. *Out of Weakness: Healing the Wounds That Lead Us to War*. Toronto: Bantam Books, 1988.

Shapiro, David. *Neurotic Styles*. New York: Basic Books, 1965.

Spencer, Laura J. *Winning Through Participation*. Dubuque, Iowa: Kendall Hunt (under the auspices of the Institute for Cultural Affairs), 1989.

Storr, Anthony. *Human Aggression*. New York: Atheneum, 1968; New York: Bantam Books, 1970.

————. *Human Destructiveness*. 1972. Reprint. New York: Grove Weidenfeld, 1991.

————. *The Integrity of the Personality*. New York: Random House, 1992.

Ulanov, Ann, and Barry Ulanov. *Cinderella and Her Sisters: The Envied and the Envying*. Philadelphia: Westminster Press, 1983.

Winnicott, Donald W. *Home Is Where We Start From: Essays by a*

Psychoanalyst. Compiled and edited by Clare Winnicott, Ray Shepherd, and Madeline Davis. New York: W. W. Norton, 1986.

Wolf, Ernest S. *Treating the Self: Elements of Clinical Self Psychology.* New York: Guilford Press, 1988.

10. *PHYSICS AND COSMOLOGY*

Editors of Time-Life Books. *Voyage Through the Universe: The Cosmos.* Alexandria, Va.: Time-Life Books, 1988.

Ferris, Timothy. *The Red Limit: The Search for the Edge of the Universe.* New York: William Morrow, 1977; New York: Bantam Books, 1977.

Morris, Richard. *Time's Arrows: Scientific Attitudes Toward Time.* New York: Simon & Schuster, 1984.

11. *PRIMATE ETHOLOGY*

Barnett, Samuel A. "Attack and Defense in Animal Societies." In *Aggression and Defense,* edited by C. D. Clemente and D. B. Lindsley. Berkeley: University of California Press, 1967.

Bourne, Geoffrey H. *Primate Odyssey.* New York: G. P. Putnam's Sons, 1974.

Desmond, Adrian J. *The Ape's Reflection.* New York: Dial Press/ James Wade, 1979.

de Wall, Frans. *Chimpanzee Politics: Power and Sex Among Apes.* New York: Harper & Row, 1982.

———. *Peacemaking Among Primates.* Cambridge: Harvard University Press, 1989.

Eibl-Eibesfeldt, Irenaus. *Biology of Peace and War: Men, Animals, and Aggression.* Translated from German by Eric Mosbacher. New York: Viking Press, 1979.

———. "The Fighting Behavior of Animals." *Scientific American* 205 (1961): 112–122.

Fossey, Diane. *Gorillas in the Mist.* Boston: Houghton Mifflin, 1983.

Goodall, Jane. *In the Shadow of Man.* Boston: Houghton Mifflin, 1971.

———. *Through a Window: My Thirty Years with the Chimpanzees of Gombe.* Boston: Houghton Mifflin, 1990.

Hall, K.R.C. "Aggression in Monkey and Ape Societies." In *The Natural History of Aggression*, edited by John D. Carthy and Francis J. Ebling. London: Academic Press (for the Institute of Biology), 1964, pp. 50–64.

Heltne, Paul G., and Linda A. Marquardt. *Understanding Chimpanzees*. Cambridge: Harvard University Press, 1989.

Matthews, L. Harrison. "Overt Fighting in Mammals." In *The Natural History of Aggression*, edited by John D. Carthy and Francis J. Ebling. London: Academic Press (for the Institute of Biology), 1964.

Morris, Desmond, and Ramona Morris. *Men and Apes*. New York: Bantam Books, 1968.

Shaw, C. E. "The Male Combat Dance of Crotalid Snakes." *Herpetologia* 4 (1948): 137–145.

Tinbergen, Niko. "Fighting and Threat in Animals." *New Biology* 14 (1953): 9–24.

12. *RITUAL AND INITIATION*

Almond, Richard. *The Healing Community: Dynamics of the Therapeutic Milieu*. Stanford: Stanford University Press, 1974.

Bellack, L., M. Hurvich, and H. Gediman. *Ego Functions in Schizophrenics, Neurotics, and Normals*. New York: John Wiley & Sons, 1973.

Benedict, Ruth. "Ritual." *Encyclopaedia of the Social Sciences* 13 (1934): 396–398.

Bossard, James A. S., and Eleanor S. Bell. "Ritual in Family Living." *American Sociological Review* 14 (1949): 463–469.

Davis, Madeleine, and David Wallbridge. *Boundary and Space: An Introduction to the Work of D. W. Winnicott*. New York: Brunner/Mazel, 1981.

Eliade, Mircea. *Rites and Symbols of Initiation: The Mysteries of Birth and Rebirth*. New York: Harper & Row, 1958.

Frank, Jerome D. *Persuasion and Healing: A Comparative Study of Psychotherapy*. New York: Schocken Books, 1963.

Gay, Volney P. "Psychopathology and Ritual: Freud's Essay 'Obsessive Actions and Religious Practices.'" *Psychoanalytic Review* 62 (1975): 493–507.

————. "Ritual and Self-Esteem in Victor Turner and Heinz Kohut."
   Zygon 18 (September 1983): 271–282.

Goodheart, William B. "Theory of Analytical Interaction." *San Francisco Jung Institute Library Journal* 1, no. 4 (1980): 2–39.

Grimes, Ronald. "Ritual Studies: Two Models." *Religious Studies
   Review* 2 (1976): 13–25.

Groesbeck, C. Jess. "The Archetypal Image of the Wounded Healer."
   The Journal of Analytical Psychology 20 (1975): 122–145.

Grolnick, Simon A., and Leonard Barkin, eds. *Between Reality and
   Fantasy: Transitional Objects and Phenomena*. New York:
   Jason Aronson, 1978.

Guggengbuhl-Craig, Adolf. *Power in the Helping Professions*. Irving,
   Tex.: Spring Publications, 1971.

Harrison, Jane. *Ancient Art and Ritual*. London: Williams & Nor-
   gate, 1913.

————. *Themis: A Study of the Social Origins of Greek Religion*.
   Cambridge: Cambridge University Press, 1912.

Hart, Onno van der. *Rituals in Psychotherapy: Transition and Conti-
   nuity*. New York: Irvington Publishers, 1983.

Langs, Robert. *The Bipersonal Field*. New York: Jason Aronson,
   1976.

————. *Interactions*. New York: Jason Aronson, 1980.

————. *Technique in Transition*. New York: Jason Aronson, 1978.

————. *The Therapeutic Environment*. New York: Jason Aronson,
   1979.

McCurdy, Alexander III. "Establishing and Maintaining the Analytical Structure." In *Jungian Analysis*, edited by Murray Stein.
   LaSalle, Ill.: Open Court, 1982.

Moore, Robert L. "Contemporary Psychotherapy as Ritual Process: An Initial Reconnaissance." *Zygon* 18 (September 1983):
   283–294.

————. "Ritual Process, Initiation, and Contemporary Religion." In
   Jung's Challenge to Contemporary Religion, edited by Murray
   Stein and Robert L. Moore. Wilmette, Ill.: Chiron Press, 1987.

————, Ralph W. Burhoe, and Philip J. Hefner, eds. "Ritual in
   Human Adaptation." Symposium reported in *Zygon* 18 (September 1983): 209–325.

Perry, John Weir. *Roots of Renewal in Myth and Madness*. San
   Francisco: Jossey-Bass, 1976.

Posinsky, S. H. "Ritual, Neurotic and Social." *American Imago* 19 (1962): 375–390.

Reik, Theodor. *Ritual: Psychoanalytic Studies*. London: Hogarth Press, 1931.

Turner, Victor. *The Drums of Affliction*. Oxford: Clarendon Press, 1968.

———. *From Ritual to Theatre*. New York: Performing Arts Journal Publications, 1982.

———. *Process, Performance and Pilgrimage: A Study in Comparative Symbology*. New Delhi: Concept Publishing, 1979.

———. *The Ritual Process: Structure and Anti-Structure*. Chicago: Aldine, 1969; Ithaca: Cornell University Press, 1969.

———, and Edith Turner. *Image and Pilgrimage in Christian Culture*. New York: Columbia University Press, 1978.

van Gennep, Arnold. *The Rites of Passage*. 1908. Reprint. Chicago: University of Chicago Press, 1960.

13. *THEOLOGY AND PHILOSOPHY*

Buber, Martin. *I and Thou*. New York: Charles Scribner's Sons, 1970.

Daley, Mary. *Beyond God the Father: Toward a Philosophy of Women's Liberation*. Boston: Beacon Press, 1973.

———. *Gyn/Ecology: The Metaethics of Radical Feminism*. Boston: Beacon Press, 1979.

de Chardin, Teilhard. *The Phenomenon of Man*. New York: Harper & Row, 1959.

Evans-Wentz, Walter Y., ed. *The Tibetan Book of the Dead*. 3d ed. New York: Oxford University Press, 1960.

Fillmore, Charles. "Jesus Christ's Atonement." In *The Unity Treasure Chest*, compiled by Lowell Fillmore, Unity School of Christianity. New York: Hawthorn Books, 1956.

Goldin, Judah. *The Living Talmud*. New Haven: Yale University Press, 1955; New York: New American Library, 1957.

Greenleaf, Robert K. *Servant Leadership: A Journey into the Nature of Legitimate Power and Greatness*. New York: Paulist Press, 1977.

Keen, Sam. *To a Dancing God: Notes of a Spiritual Traveler*. San Francisco: Harper & Row, 1970.

Kelly, J.N.D. *Early Christian Doctrines*. 2d ed. New York: Harper & Row, 1960.

Kelly, Sean. *Individuation and the Absolute: Hegel, Jung, and the Path Toward Wholeness*. New York: Paulist Press, 1993.

Kirk, G. S., and J. E. Raven. *The Presocratic Philosophers: A Critical History with a Selection of Texts*. Cambridge: Cambridge University Press, 1957.

Loye, David. *The Sphinx and the Rainbow: Brain, Mind, and Future Vision*. Boston: Shambhala, 1983.

Nicholas of Cusa. *The Vision of God*. Translated by O. R. Gurney. Edited by Evelyn Underhill. New York: Ungar, 1960.

Niebuhr, Reinhold. *The Nature and Destiny of Man: A Christian Interpretation*. Vol. 1. New York: Charles Scribner's Sons, 1941, 1964.

Nikhilananda, Swami. *The Upanishads*. New York: Ramakrishna-Vivekananda Center, 1949.

Nilsson, Martin P. *Greek Piety*. Translated from Swedish by Herbert J. Rose. 1948. Reprint. New York: W. W. Norton, 1969.

Norris, Richard A., Jr., and William G. Rusch, eds. *The Christological Controversy*. Translated by Richard A. Norris. Philadelphia: Fortress Press, 1980.

Pickthall, Marmaduke. *The Meaning of the Glorious Koran*. New York: New American Library, 1953.

Pirsig, Robert M. *Zen and the Art of Motorcycle Maintenance*. Toronto: Bantam Books, 1975.

Plato. *Apology, Crito, Phaedo, Symposium, Republic*. Translated by Benjamin Jowett. Edited with introduction by Louise R. Loomis. Roslyn, N.Y.: Walter J. Black, 1942.

Prabhupada, A. C. Bhaktivedanta Swami. *Bhagavad-Gita As It Is*. New York: Macmillan/Collier Books, 1972.

Ruether, Rosemary R. *Sexism and God-Talk: Toward a Feminist Theology*. Boston: Beacon Press, 1973.

Tillich, Paul. *The Courage to Be*. New Haven: Yale University Press, 1952.

———. *The Eternal Now*. New York: Charles Scribner's Sons, 1963.

———. *Systematic Theology*. Vol. 3. Part 4: *Life and the Spirit* and Part 5: *History and the Kingdom of God*. Chicago: University of Chicago Press, 1963. Especially Chapter 1 of Part 4, "Life, Its Ambiguities, and the Quest for Unambiguous Life," and Chapter 3 of Part 5, "The Kingdom of God as the End of History."

Watts, Alan. *The Supreme Identity: An Essay on Oriental Meta-physic and the Christian Religion*. New York: Random House/Vintage, 1972.

Wei, Henry. *The Guiding Light of Lao Tze*. Wheaton, Ill.: Theosophical Publishing House, 1982.

Whitehead, Alfred North. *Adventures of Ideas*. 1933. Reprint. New York: Free Press, 1967.

———. *Process and Reality: An Essay in Cosmology*. New York: Free Press, 1978.

14. AUDIOTAPES

These audiotapes may be ordered from the C. G. Jung Institute of Chicago, 1567 Maple St., Evanston, Ill. 60201; (708) 475-4848, fax (708) 475-4970.

Robert Moore

Archetypal Images of the King and Warrior

Archetypal Images of the Magician and Lover

The Ego and Its Relations with the Unconscious, 2 tapes

The Four Couples Within: The Structure of the Self and the Dynamics of Relationship, 3 tapes

Healing the Masculine

Jihad: The Archetype of Spiritual Warfare

Jungian Psychology and Human Spirituality: Liberation from Tribalism in Religious Life, 5 tapes

The King Within: A Study in Masculine Psychology, 7 tapes

The Liminoid and the Liminal

The Lover Within: A Study in Masculine Psychology, 8 tapes

The Magician Within: A Study in Masculine Psychology, 4 tapes

Masculine Power: Archetypal Potential and Planetary Challenge

The Meaning of Sacred Space in Transformation

Narcissism and Human Evil

The Nature of Sacred Space

Portraits of Crisis: Experience and Theory, 2 tapes

The Psychology of Satan: Encountering the Dark Side of the Self, 8 tapes

Rediscovering Masculine Potentials, 4 tapes

Rediscovering the Mature Masculine: Resources from Archetypal Psychology, 3 tapes

Ritual, Initiation, and Contemporary Religion
The Trickster Archetype: Potential and Pathology, 3 tapes
The Vessel of Analysis
The Warrior Within: A Study in Masculine Psychology, 5 tapes
Robert Moore and Forrest Craver
Dancing the Four Quarters: Visions of Grassroots Masculine Leadership in the 1990s
Robert Moore and Douglas Gillette
King, Warrior, Magician, Lover: Rediscovering the Archetypes of the Mature Masculine
Robert Moore and Michael Meade
The Great Self Within: Men and the Quest for Significance
Robert Moore and Caroline Stevens
The One and the Two: Gender, Identity and Relationship. 8 tapes

INDEX

Grateful acknowledgment is made to the following individuals and publishers for permission to reproduce material used in creating the figures in this book. Every effort has been made to locate the copyright holders of material used here. Omissions brought to our attention will be corrected in future editions.

p. 49: The Jung Foundation (reproduced from Edward Edinger, *Ego and Archetype* [New York: Penguin Books, 1974]).

p. 50 (top): Dr. Pedro Rojas (reproduced from *The Art and Architecture of Mexico from 10000 B.C. to the Present Day*).

p. 51 (top): British Museum, Honolulu (reproduced from Joseph Campbell, *The Mythic Image* [Princeton: Princeton University Press, 1974]); (bottom): University of Chicago Press.

p. 57: Baron Hugo Van Lawick.

p. 59: Houghton Mifflin Company for Lovers in Paradise: Heart to Heart at Gombe from *In the Shadow of Man.*

p. 64: The Viking Press for The Garden of Immortality: Phallus as the Tree of Life from *The Masks of God: Occidental Mythology.*

p. 70: Penguin Books, Inc. for Mamallapuram: Shrine with Ligam from *The Axis of Eros.*

p. 72: The Camelot Press for Dionysus Enraptured: A State of Ecstasy from *The Clashing Rocks: Early Greek Religion and Culture and the Origins of Drama.*

p. 78: Doubleday & Co. for Friendship Love: Men Risking Their Lives for Other Men from *The Power of Myth.*

p. 82: Penguin Books for In the Garden: Krishna and Radha Embracing from *Axis of Eros.*

p. 85: Grove Press for Avalokiteśvara: Bodhisatvas and Universal Love from *The Wonder That Was India.*

p. 89: Doubleday & Co. for The Cult of Romantic Love from *The Power of Myth.*

p. 93: Doubleday & Co. for Mother and Son: The Owl Goddess and the Dependent Male from *The Power of Myth.*

p. 96: Harper & Row for The Aroused Lover: Nikkie's Invitation to a Female from *Chipanzee Politics: Power and Sex Among Apes.*

p. 100: Grolier Inc. for The Effemanite Christ (*The Baptism of Christ*, Masolino, 1435) from *Las Bellas Artes, Volumen 2, El Arte Italiano Hasta 1850.*

p. 104: Penguin Books for Krishna and the Gopis from *Axis of Eros.*

p. 107: *Life* magazine for The Outlaw Lover: Marlon Brando from the Fall 1990 issue.

p. 111: Penguin Books for The Lover and His Beloved in the Garden: Krishna and Radha in Amorous Embrace from *Axis of Eros.*

p. 114: Indiana University Press for The Musician Embodying the Lover: Nyama Suso Reciting with *Kora* Accompaniment from *Africa.*

p. 115: Doubleday & Co. for The Pool—Apache: The Lover at One with Nature (Edward S. Curtis, 1868–1952) from *The Power of Myth.*

p. 117: Doubleday & Co. for Jackson Pollock: The Artist Embodying the Lover from *Man and His Symbols.*

p. 129: Rudolph Vetter for Ecstatic Embrace.

p. 131: Collier Books/Macmillan Publishing Co. for I and Thou from *Erotic Spirituality: The Vision of Konarak.*

p. 136: Vendome Press for For the Lover, Life Is a Carnival from *The Joy of Rio.*

p. 138: Doubleday & Co. for The Spiritualizing Lover: At One with the Cosmos from *Man and His Symbols.*

p. 141: Doubleday & Co. for The Mysterious Anima: Goddess of Fertility, Bread, and the Crescent Moon from *Man and His Symbols.*

p. 142: Doubleday & Co. for The Lover as Visionary (*Moses* by Marc Chagall) from *The Power of Myth.*

p. 145: Grolier Inc. for The Lover as Radical Incarnation (*The Annunciation* by Ludovico Carracci, 1585) from *Las Bellas Artes: Volumen 2: El Arte Italiano Hasta 1850.*

p. 147: University of Chicago Press for The Divine Within the Material: The Epiphany of Hathor Among the Papyrus from *Kingship and the Gods: A Study of Ancient Near Eastern Religion as the Integration of Society and Nature.*

p. 151: Doubleday & Co. for The Lover as the Agent of Social Change: Martin Luther King, Jr., from *The Power of Myth.*

p. 154: Doubleday & Co. for The Lover as Generative Man: Caring for Future Generations from *Man and His Symbols.*